# FOSTER
## PARENTING
### STEP-BY-STEP

*of related interest*

**Life Story Work with Children Who Are Fostered or Adopted**
**Creative Ideas and Activities**
*Katie Wrench and Lesley Naylor*
ISBN 978 1 84905 343 3
eISBN 978 0 85700 674 5

**Attachment in Common Sense and Doodles**
**A Practical Guide**
*Miriam Silver*
*Doodles by Teg Lansdell*
ISBN 978 1 84905 314 3
eISBN 978 0 85700 624 0

**Reparenting the Child Who Hurts**
**A Guide to Healing Developmental Trauma and Attachments**
*Caroline Archer and Christine Gordon*
*Foreword by Gregory C. Keck, PhD.*
ISBN 978 1 84905 263 4
eISBN 978 0 85700 568 7

**Direct Work with Vulnerable Children**
**Playful Activities and Strategies for Communication**
*Audrey Tait and Helen Wosu*
*Foreword by Brigid Daniel*
ISBN 978 1 84905 319 8
eISBN 978 0 85700 661 5

**Creating Loving Attachments**
**Parenting with PACE to Nurture Confidence and Security**
**in the Troubled Child**
*Kim S. Golding and Daniel A. Hughes*
ISBN 978 1 84905 227 6
eISBN 978 0 85700 470 3

**Empathic Behaviour Management For Foster and Adoptive Families**
*Amber Elliott*
ISBN 9781849053396
eISBN 978 0 85700 671 4

**A Short Introduction to Attachment and Attachment Disorder**
*Colby Pearce*
ISBN 978 1 84310 957 0
eISBN 978 1 84642 949 1
JKP Short Introductions Series

**Nurturing Attachments**
**Supporting Children Who Are Fostered or Adopted**
*Kim S. Golding*
ISBN 978 1 84310 614 2
eISBN 978 1 84642 750 3

# FOSTER
## PARENTING
## STEP-BY-STEP

How to Nurture the Traumatized
Child and Overcome Conflict

DR. KALYANI GOPAL

Foreword by Irene Clements

Jessica Kingsley *Publishers*
London and Philadelphia

First published in 2013
by Jessica Kingsley Publishers
116 Pentonville Road
London N1 9JB, UK
and
400 Market Street, Suite 400
Philadelphia, PA 19106, USA

*www.jkp.com*

Copyright © Kalyani Gopal 2013
Foreword copyright © Irene Clements 2013

**Library of Congress Cataloging in Publication Data**
A CIP catalog record for this book is available from the Library of Congress

**British Library Cataloguing in Publication Data**
A CIP catalogue record for this book is available from the British Library

ISBN 978 1 84905 937 4
eISBN 978 0 85700 751 3

Printed and bound in Great Britain

*This book is dedicated to all those foster families I have had the privilege to treat, without whom I would not have learned what is shared in these pages.*

*I was very fortunate in having a wonderful childhood thanks to my parents' unconditional love and my grandmother.*

*This book is especially dedicated to my children, who have trained me as only children can.*

# CONTENTS

# FOREWORD

How often over the last 30-seen years and now in my role as President of the National Foster Parent Association have I heard these words: "If only I had known, I would have parented differently?" How many times did I say that myself over the 27 years my husband and I fostered? We had so much to learn back in the 1970s about fostering and very little was available to assist us as we learned of the uniqueness of each child we welcomed into our home—127 incredible children with more needs than we could begin to comprehend.

We did not have a clue as to how to parent so many diverse children with so many diverse needs. We talked with other foster parents when we could find them, we talked to doctors and teachers and social workers. It was frightening that there appeared to be neither an organized network to utilize for teaching/learning and information nor a network to provide supports and services to foster parents and the children in their care.

Where were the books, videos, tapes, trainings, support groups, etc. that we needed to help us even begin to feel equipped to meet such varying and often extreme needs? Sad to say, the selection was slim to none. So, people who opened their families and homes to other people's children flew solo most of the time, often begging for insights and assistance from state workers who were ill prepared to help in any significant manner.

Over the years many things changed. Research was conducted on the needs and behaviors of children entering and in foster care and books and videos began to be published to assist caregivers. Organized training sessions and relevant curriculums were developed and published. Local and state foster parent associations were started to provide training and supports to foster parents. The National Foster Parent Association was organized to provide supports and services and to serve as the National Voice of Foster Parents.

When asked to read Dr. Gopal's new book and provide this Foreword for the book, I did not hesitate. Dr. Gopal has been a lifeline for many children in foster care and their parents and foster parents for many years. Dr. Gopal is also a well-known speaker and has blessed the National Foster Parent Association with numerous workshop presentations at our annual education conferences. Her dedication to providing information that works is key and most appreciated by all who hear her or read her books.

In *Foster Parenting Step-by-Step: How to Nurture the Traumatized Child and Overcome Conflict*, Dr. Gopal uses a style of writing that is more conversational that formal. She writes as if she were sitting across the table from you and explaining the incredibly many aspects of foster care and foster parenting. My recommendation is to read the book from cover to cover, taking time to mark those areas that you know you will want to refer to time and time again as you welcome additional children into your home. This new book provides insights and recommendations that will be beneficial to all who choose to provide foster care and/or kinship care.

*Irene Clements*
*President, National Foster Parent Association*

# QUOTES FROM FOSTER CHILDREN

"Don't take away my memories; they make me who I am."

"Sometimes I dream that my mother is dead in some alley, and I will never see her again."

"I can't sleep at night; there are buggy eyes watching me."

"My mama, she is supposed to take care of me, that is her job, not you, I guess she just don't care."

"My mama, she chooses her boyfriends over us, she says she loves us but she don't—not that much."

"When I got taken from my mama, I hated everybody and did not care; I was real bad."

"My mama, she tells me to steal checks from the neighbors' mail then she gives me a dollar for candy."

"I took care of my little brothers and sisters, my mama would wake me up at night when she left, I was six years old."

"It is my fault my brother died in the closet, it should have been me who was tied and beat, I'm older. I couldn't wake him up."

"My mama, she made me go to the store and get her cigarettes after she stuck the knife in my uncle."

"My mama locked my brother and me in the room and we banged on the door and when it didn't open, we used it in the garbage can. Then she whooped us."

"I want to have a baby so there's somebody to love me no matter what."

"My wrists and feet were tied to the bed, and when they were high they laughed and whooped us."

"My dad made me sleep on the hard floor at night in the hallway. And in the morning he whooped me if I used it [urinated] on myself at night. The floor was cold in the winter."

"I have this mark from Daddy Rat, and this one here is from Baby Rat. I think the others are from…I don't know, we had roaches and rats."

"When I was being bad, my mama would hang me over the top of the roof. I tried to scream but was too scared."

"My stepdad told me he was going to teach me how to be grown so I would be smarter than the boys."

"He told me if I told, he would kill my mom."

"I let him touch me so he would leave my little sister alone. But he broke his promise. Why did he do that to her? I was good, I did everything."

"I tried to hold my sister, he was hitting me so hard, she fell… I miss her."

"My mama told me she regretted not keeping her legs closed so she would not have had me; I told her why didn't you?"

"I did not tell anyone because it would make my mama sad; she loves him."

"My mama gave us away so we could eat."

"Nobody understands, my mama is a really good person, they say such mean things."

"I don't know why I do that. Why do I pull my hair?"

"My dad burned my sister on the chest, he took a spoon and he put fire on it."

"I didn't look all the way, and I ran, and ran and ran, and I only saw the long part, and she told me that it didn't happen."

"I was on fire one day, because my daddy light the mattress 'coz I was sleep and he tell me to wake up and I didn't want to."

# PREFACE

*"If I believe I cannot do something, it makes me incapable of doing it. But when I believe I can, then I acquire the ability to do it even if I didn't have it in the beginning."*
—Mahatma Gandhi

*"First, have a definite, clear practical ideal; a goal, an objective. Second, have the necessary means to achieve your ends; wisdom, money, materials, and methods. Third, adjust all your means to that end."*
—Aristotle

This book is written on behalf of all those wonderful and dear foster children that I have had the privilege to meet and treat over the past 25 years, and to those foster parents whose confusion and sadness have demonstrated the need for me to write this book.

There are quite a few books of this nature on the shelves, or available for download as ebooks from the internet, but none speak about the "nitty gritty" how-to details in a way that can actually help our foster parents and children bond and live with one another. In this book, foster parents are provided with a rationale for keeping their foster children, the dos and don'ts of parenting skills, how to maneuver the maze of new parenting skills required to parent these children, how to cope with their failures, and how to seek help from resources.

The bane of human existence lies in the multitude of negative human experiences that each of us go through in life. Some of us are more resilient than others, some are harder and more bitter than others. Our children do not have that veneer of protection from their worlds, because their worlds are us. Love, warmth, kindness, affection, and understanding are the deepest ties that bond us to our offspring. When we as parents abuse this bond, we permanently impair our children's capacities to attach and grow into healthy adults, leaving foster parents to pick up the pieces.

Disruptions in the attachment bonds result in difficulties with subsequent adjustment in life due to developmental changes that take place in the brain, and in the external environment. In the United States alone, a 2002 study revealed that 49 percent of those incarcerated had been in the foster care system. A recent study in Australia found that 73 percent of infants and children in foster care had attachment-related behavior problems.[1] They lag behind their same-age peers by a year or more in school and even more in terms of their emotional and behavioral controls. They find it difficult to keep jobs. Our kids who have "graduated" from foster care make up at least 16 percent of the homeless population in the United States and 67 percent in the UK. The sudden lack of freedom, absence of benevolent authority figures who surrounded them throughout their childhood and adolescence, and loss of all contact with their biological families leaves them destitute and impoverished.

So how can we change the lives of our future generations in foster care placements? This book is a small attempt in that direction, a step in the journey to reduce changes in placements after struggling to raise uncontrollable and unloving foster children. In the life of an average defiant, angry, and acting-out foster child, there are often five to nine changes in foster care placements at a minimum, with multiple hospitalizations, residential treatment placements, respite care, teen group home placements, and finally transitioning into independent living where they either learn to swim and succeed, or drown in the abyss of poverty, drugs, prostitution, and homelessness.

This book is all about empowerment. Successful foster parents are those who can handle a wide variety of behaviors and emotions. By empowering our foster parents to be more successful, we empower our foster children to heal and increase their future chances of succeeding in life, thereby breaking the cycle of abuse and neglect from their biological family. A change in one family changes the lives of its subsequent generations.

The second goal of this book is to address future directions in the foster care system. I write from my own experiences living and working in the USA, but know that the same issues affect families and care systems worldwide, so I will try to write in universal terms that will translate to the reader, wherever you live.

The 2011 United States statistics show that children in immigrant families make up 23 percent of the population[2] and their families' parenting practices differ depending on their country of origin's parenting practices. An international approach to foster parenting will therefore be addressed, especially within the first few chapters.

## Notes

1. Chambers *et al.* 2010.
2. Kidscount 2011.

# INTRODUCTION

## The foster care system

Each year, many children enter the foster care system. In the United States alone around 200,000 to 300,000 new children enter each year with 10 percent of their parents being terminated from parental rights. In other countries, as many as 50–90 percent of their "looked after" children (LAC) are also placed in foster care rather than orphanages.[1] The foster care predicament is an international concern.

While the relevant statistics, processes, and legal requirements relating to foster care differ from country to country (and often state to state within countries), there are overarching priorities shared by all foster carers, such as a recognition of the need to provide supportive and understanding care to the child in their care.

There are also shared challenges: how to respond to severe behavioral problems, how to encourage bonding, and how to understand the impact of early trauma on the child. Such problems are commonly addressed by doctors who neglect their root causes.

## Managing challenging behaviors

For example, in the United States in 2008, the government paid 288.8 million dollars in medication costs for children under the age of 18. Texas has since cut the percentage of their children on medication from 30 percent to 17 percent after tracking medication in their foster children. A Rutgers University study[2] that examined the use of medication in 16 US states showed that children in foster care are nine times more likely to be placed on medication than other children.

However, in many cases, medication alone does not work in addressing problem behavior, and as these children grow up they are unresponsive to their medications. Childhood behaviors stemming from trauma, neglect, abuse, and disruption of attachment are all treated routinely with medication while the root causes—the absence of secure attachment for most children, and the many disruptions in the development of their brain—are ignored or under-treated.

## Displacement trauma and coping mechanisms

Foster children may be removed from their parents' care at any hour of the day or night, often confused and bewildered, and bundled into a car with a few belongings shoved into a garbage or plastic bag. Law enforcement personnel come to their homes and take them from their parents' care. Well-meaning law enforcement agents performing their duty to protect our children from harm then contribute to the traumatic memories of these children that are repeatedly seen in psychological protocol.

Due to this phenomenon of "displacement trauma" children in foster care develop a unique set of coping mechanisms that make them fall into four major categories: the "pleasers," "distancers," "rejecters," and "changers." I will explain these categories in more detail later in the book.

## Foster parents

Typically, foster parents enter into foster parenting with a variety of motives. They go through seven major stages during the time they spend with each new foster child. These comprise the following:

1. motivational
2. planning

3. welcoming

4. adapting

5. educational

6. empowering

7. disengaging/adopting.

The dilemma of foster parenting is to give nurturing and protection during the child's residence at their home, but then disengage and detach after the child is gone—not an easy feat to achieve; the mental health and stability of the foster parent is therefore critical for the adjustment of the child in their home.

In the chapters that follow, I aim to provide step-by-step guidance to some of the difficult choices and issues you might expect to face as a foster carer, provide you with information to help you to understand foster children, and advise on how best to respond to challenging behavior. In Chapter 1 I will take you through the initial journey of the foster parenting experience to help you decide whether or not foster parenting is suited to your needs. I will cover the jargon relating to foster care used in different countries, and will consider their unique approaches and common ways of dealing with the human condition. My hope is that no matter where you live and work in the world, you will find the learning techniques and knowledge provided throughout this book useful.

Chapter 2 covers the importance of planning and knowing whether you are ready to become a foster parent. The goal is to help you prevent common errors with your own children and family which well-meaning foster parents can make when going through the process, and which can lead to huge regrets and heartache later on.

In Chapter 3, you will learn what to ask and how to welcome a sad and frightened child into your home; you will also learn how to use all your social support systems to help ease the child's transition into your home while protecting your own family.

The concept of "displacement trauma," which I have developed over the years to explain the unique coping mechanisms that foster children develop, will be outlined in Chapter 4, so that you can grasp why, no matter how much love, structure, and guidance you provide, your foster children maintain their own unique ways of coping.

In Chapter 5, the importance of bonding is discussed, with emphasis on how to show love in a way that the child is willing to accept. Most foster children have strong loyalties to their family of origin and foster parents often make grievous errors in handling this delicate issue.

Chapter 6 revolves around parenting, and education about the many facets of foster parenting and mental disorders commonly diagnosed in foster children, so that you can be well informed even before seeing the child's therapist and social worker.

Chapter 7 covers state-of-the-art parenting strategies that have been found to be effective for foster children. In this chapter, I combine my own clinical experiences of training over 5000 foster parents with the literature on parenting to provide some key advice to help you.

Chapter 8 is the final chapter that deals with the most painful process—the part where you will need to let this child leave the safety of your home, possibly to the unstable biological home that you have zero control over. I will share with you ways in which you might be allowed to provide a respite for the biological mother and so stay in the child's life—it's all about giving the biological mother a sense of security about her own role in her child's life.

Finally, to conclude the book I have featured a range of resources, "go to" websites and related articles of interest for those who want to find out more, or who are looking for more information relating to their own local area or country. There is a huge amount of information out there, and it can be confusing to professionals, let alone parents. In writing this book, I found over 15,000 peer-reviewed articles and books, but for the purposes of the book I have narrowed it down to a highly selective bibliography should you wish to explore further and gain more knowledge.

## Note to the reader

This book is intended to be a useful, quick guide, which focuses primarily on relationships, parenting, and the needs of the child in foster care—subjects that are universal.

Inevitably, writing as I do from the perspective of a US citizen with experience of the US system, there is a bias within this book. For the most part, though, the content of this book relates to all foster carers. However, in some sections which relate to the law or school systems, it is beyond the scope of this book to provide full details for every country so I have instead provided links where further information can be found.

## Notes

1. Kjeldsen 2010; Wolf 2008; Woo *et al.* 2007; Byrne *et al.* 2004; Chipungu and Bent-Goodley 2004; Peake and Townsend 2012.
2. Medicaid Medical Directors Learning Network and Rutgers Center for Education and Research on Mental Health Therapeutics 2010.

# CHAPTER 1

# THE MOTIVATIONAL STAGE

First Things First! Know What to Expect

## The foster parent experience

This guide has been written to empower you as foster parents to succeed in raising your foster children.

"Foster parents" is the term I will use throughout this book for the sake of simplicity, though in other countries the same role might be described as "resource parents," "foster carers," or "professional carers."

It is my hope that in reading this book, you will learn how to achieve situation-specific healthy parenting control, mobilize resource skills, and achieve confidence in your ability to raise someone else's child.

As a foster parent, your foster child is being shared with you for a limited period of time. You are going to or have become the "caretaker" parent. You may be mentally willing to accept the child, heal the spirit, and give abundant love, but when this child arrives they do not want to live with you. You can expect delays in development and maturity, and a lack of ability to handle day-to-day stress. These children have come from neglectful or abusive homes, and are generally lacking in love, protection, nurturing, warmth, and food. Many children have not heard of the rules that you consider important and necessary. Food, love, safety, and shelter are basic necessities that they do not take for granted.

The dilemma of foster parenting is to develop attachment and bond to the child when he or she arrives and then have the skill to detach when they leave.

## Reasons why children enter foster care

There are several reasons why children enter foster care. Some of the major ones are:

- mental illness affecting the caretaking parent
- death of a parent
- loss of housing, shelter, incarceration of parent
- physical or sexual abuse of the child
- abandonment by the parent
- drug abuse/addiction leading to absence of the parent
- lack of food, water, and basic necessities
- inability of the parent to ensure education access
- inability of the parent to take care of the child due to mental retardation or physical illness.

However, the vast majority of children enter foster care due to neglect. So what is neglect?

An excellent definition is: "Neglect is the persistent failure to meet a child's basic physical and/or psychological needs, likely to result in the serious impairment of the child's health or development."[1]

Neglect can be:

- physical
- medical
- emotional
- educational.

Failure to protect a child from harm such as sexual or physical abuse is another reason why children enter into foster care. In the USA, such abuse is included in the definition under Federal Law[2] (CAPTA) in which child abuse and neglect is:

any recent act or failure to act on the part of a parent or caretaker which results in death, serious physical or emotional harm, sexual abuse or exploitation

or

an act or failure to act which presents an imminent risk of serious harm.

When parents fail to feed their child, lock them in their bedrooms for days with no food or water, beat them severely, allow strangers or family members to sexually hurt them, refuse to enforce school attendance, and fail to provide them with their basic needs, all of these constitute child abuse and/or neglect irrespective of the part of the world we live in. It is in situations such as these that the help of foster parents is critical.

And, in turn, this book—like many others—is written to help you transform this hurt child's life by teaching you effective parenting skills and supporting your journey. Whether you live in Louisiana or London, Arizona or Africa, children are children and their basic needs are fairly similar across the oceans.

Broadly, five areas or "domains" have been found to be the most important areas of the foster parents' experience, as shown in Table 1.1.[3] Check (✓) all examples that apply to you and discuss these with your social worker, family, and peers.

**Table 1.1 Five domains of foster parents' experience**

| Domain | Positive experience | Negative experience | |
|---|---|---|---|
| Birth family | Enriching experience | Hated the birth family | ☐ |
| Motivation | Now want more children | Worried about "our" safety | ☐ |
| Agency influences | Liked social worker | No stability, many changes | ☐ |
| Family relationships | Empathy and kindness | My own children resented her | ☐ |
| Attachment | Like one of my own | I feel confused and rejected | ☐ |

## Motives for becoming a foster parent

Studies[4] have shown that the reasons for becoming foster parents include:

- wanting to make a difference in the life of a child
- wanting to help more children (foster parents with community concerns are six times more likely to have secure attachments with infants)
- supplement family income
- wanting to have more children
- sympathy
- wanting their children to learn to share, have company
- wanting to give love to children
- empty-nesters.

If your motivation is that you are empty-nesters, then becoming foster parents to infants is not recommended. On the other hand, a strong love for children is excellent for developing secure attachment in infants.

## Qualities of successful foster parents

Research suggests[5] that successful foster parents have in common at least some of the following ten characteristics:

1. ability to work as a team
2. capacity to provide a nurturing and caring environment
3. desire to be a parent linked to own inability to conceive children
4. identification with the child due to own history of maltreatment
5. emotional stability
6. love of children
7. ability to handle a wide range of behavioral disorders
8. extensive training in foster care

9. great self-awareness of prejudices, beliefs, and values

10. transcultural parenting confidence.

## Importance of placement stability in a foster home

The first six months is the time of highest risk for placement stability for 70 percent of children[6] due to adjustment issues that can jeopardize foster families. For example, in the United States, 33 percent of children who returned home in 2010 had an average length of stay in foster care of less than 12 months.[7]

There are three levels of stability in placement within the first 18 months.[8] These are:

- early stability: same placement for 45 days
- late stability: same placement beyond 45 days
- unstable placement.

In turn, children can be categorized into risk levels for placement instability:

- low risk
- medium risk
- high risk.

Placement stability can be explained as the length of time that a child and foster parent successfully adapt to one another and the child remains in the foster home. In the UK, for example, for children in foster care for at least two and a half years, placement stability is measured by:[9]

- fewer than three placements in a year
- at least one placement of two years.

## The jargon of the foster care experience: what do these terms mean?

- *Foster parent.* An individual who takes in a child into their home by virtue of being given permission by the child welfare authorities in their region of residence. Foster parents are also known as "resource parents" (Child Welfare League of America), "foster carers" (UK), or "professional carers" (Denmark).[10]

- *Social worker.* Also known as "case manager" in North America and South America.

- *Foster child.* The child who has been identified as a CHINS case (USA) or a CIN (UK), which means a Child in Need of Services. The child's legal guardian is the regional authority which may be the state, country, department, or ministry. Foster children are also referred to as "looked after" children (UK).

- *Agency.* Also known as "local authority," the organization that provides oversight for foster parents and is responsible for compliance with the rules and regulations governing the care of foster children. You as a foster parent will be trained by the agency that enrolled you and can continue to receive training from the larger government organization that funds your agency.

- *Visitation.* By law, biological families have the right to visit their biological children during the period they are in foster care. The reasons are mainly to protect the parent/child bond as much as possible, to help the family heal and get back together, and to motivate the parents to work hard to get their children back. Foster care is meant to be temporary until proven otherwise.

- *Termination of parental rights.* Every state, county, and country has a set of rules pertaining to compliance of biological parents with the court requirements. In the United States, when parents are unable or unwilling to comply, visitation will cease and their rights will be terminated by the court. For example, if a mother continues to abuse drugs heavily and has "dirty drops" (positive drug/alcohol presence in urine tests, a term commonly used in the US), her rights will be terminated after a stated period of time due to noncompliance with the case plan.

- *Case plan.* A plan agreed upon by the regional authorities regarding how the child should be taken care of, the treatment plan, visitations, and reunification plan with the parent(s).

- *Foster parent organization.* Once you have decided to be a foster parent, sign up for a local association and get the support you will need during your months and years of foster parenting. These organizations hold seminars, continuing education, and conferences every year and invite speakers to provide training in areas of concern and interest. Foster parent associations around the world represent your needs and concerns. Joining your local foster parent organization is strongly recommended, as it will give you support and help with your training and fostering needs. You will find a list of foster parent associations at the back of this book.

## Stages of development of foster parenting

It is useful to identify which stage you as a foster parent are currently in. This will assist the social worker in selecting the best fit between child and parent, identifying additional skills that need to be developed for the parent, and ensuring ongoing professional skill development. There are four stages in the development of foster parenting (Table 1.2).[11]

**Table 1.2 Levels of development of foster parenting**

| Stage | Expectations and needs | Tasks | Success indicators |
|---|---|---|---|
| I Pre-contact | Naïve, enthusiastic, confident, hopeful, trusting, sympathetic | Orientation: willing to take training and give support; program policies | Self-disclosure; responsibilities |
| II Contact | Confusion, anxiety, feelings of inadequacy; criticism of program; self-doubt; desire to withdraw from fostering | Able to voice; ask for help; follow directions; modify parenting style; implement structure | Positive response; frequent phone calls to case managers; views help as constructive; follows daily routines; demonstrates interest |
| III Stabilization | Realistic confidence; use their "gut" feeling; self-doubt and correction; decreased need for agency support; client-centered; experimentation; generational boundaries established | More autonomy; reduced dependency on agency; ability to share control; client-centered attitude and behaviors; effective discipline | Increase in: developing plans; designing BM (Behavior Modification) plans; self-reliance |
| IV Collegial | Sharing with agency; increased skills lead to personal growth; open communication; increased respect for experts in the field | Act responsibly; interact very easily with peers/agency; use constructive criticism; maintain supportive attitude; maintain client focus | Empathy; openness; attention to quality; separates personal and professional issues; creative and candid approach; shares emotions and events |

## Role of cultural values in placement success

According to clinical experience and literature, there are six areas that are commonly identified as being very important for placement success:

1. Self-awareness of one's own beliefs and values. For example, "How do I really feel about having a (white, black, Hispanic) kid in my home? What do we think about that race?"

2. Participation in activities typical of that culture/ community activities.

3. Training in cultural diversity and competencies.

4. Cross-cultural support.

5. Agency support.

6. Positive past exposure to other cultures leading to tolerance, acceptance, openness.

### *Cultures and parent/child relationships*

The way foster parents express themselves to their children affects their child's sense of self-esteem and competence.

There are three types of parental expressive behaviors, also called "parental expressivity," which differ between and within cultures. These are:

1. *Positive parental expressivity:* Gratitude, laughing, smiling, encouraging, warmth.

2. *Negative dominant:* Hostility, anger, contempt, blaming.

3. *Negative submissive:* Apologizing, sadness, shame, embarrassment.

## Relationship between parenting style and social competence[12]

It is important to note that while parenting styles differ across cultures, certain styles have a negative impact on the child's development. Across both eastern and western cultures, for example Chinese, Indonesian, European and American, long-term studies have found:

Authoritarian style of parenting (inflexible) + Negative dominant parenting = Child acting-out behaviors

Authoritative style of parenting (accepting) + Positive parenting = Socially competent child

## *Strategies that work to enhance cross-cultural comfort*

- Openly talk about race and cultural differences with the child.
- Ask the agency to identify other families in similar situations so that you can build a support network.
- Attend group sessions, which are helpful to identify confusion or concerns. Increased training in cultural competence also helps foster parents understand cultural similarities.
- Spend time with the child's birth family/extended family.
- Visit the community the child came from.
- Read about the history of the child's ethnic background with the child and with other foster and biological children.
- Develop a sense of pride in the child about her/his ethnic background.
- Facilitate positive experiences with birth and extended family, community, and cultural background for the child.

It would be helpful if agencies in an area identified specific individuals within an ethnic background to be the "supportive community resource persons" for cross-cultural families. This way, a newly cross-cultural family can be eased into the adjustment period without having to reinvent the wheel and find new resources.

## Kinship versus non-kinship foster parenting

Since the 1980s, relative foster care placement or "kinship care" has gained momentum in the west, although this approach to child care has been in place for a long time in many cultures around the world. The argument for kinship placement relates to familiarity with one's birth family, the comfort of belonging, and the ability to continue to have contact with the birth family and maintain cultural identity.[13] However, the flip side of this argument has been that if the parents are neglectful or abusive, then how can we guarantee that their own families are not also neglectful or abusive? Furthermore, generational boundaries are harder to establish when placed in relative foster homes due to the relationship of the foster child with cousins, grandparents, aunts, and uncles. There are three types of kinship care:

1. *Informal care:* No court involvement.

2. *Voluntary care:* Where parents ask for help.

3. *Formal care or legal placement:* Placed by courts.

The majority of children in relative foster care are placed with their grandparents (48%), or their aunt/uncle (44%), with "others" comprising 8 percent. Most of these children are placed with the mother's side of the family (73%) rather than the father's (27%).

Generations United (www.gu.org) is a social organization that supports kinship care and is an excellent resource for grandparents and relatives. In collaboration with the Brookdale Foundation, they have developed KinNET as a resource for kinship foster families in the United States.

Characteristics of kinship or "family and friends" foster homes are:

- older parents
- fewer out-of-home placements
- greater contact with biological parents
- children remain in their own community
- lower household income than non-kinship (in general)
- single-parent household
- parents tend to be more supportive with termination
- more stable mental health due to well-maintained family relationships and protective ties
- less stigma by peers
- lowered risk of mental illness
- greater happiness among the children in need of care.[14]

African Americans tend to be disproportionately represented in the foster care system in the United States,[15] and in the UK black and minority ethnic children are also over-represented, with the largest groups having one or both parents with an African Caribbean or African heritage. African American children in kinship foster homes have been found to succeed far more than those in traditional foster homes, especially when they had:

- higher degree of structure in the home
- clear boundaries—what you can and cannot do
- clear roles and expectations.

In Native American children and in tribal populations such as the Aborigines in West Australia, kinship care is vital in maintaining cultural heritage and identity.[16]

## Risks of kinship foster homes

Risks presented by kinship care foster homes include:

- less help and support from social agencies

- less access to mental health agencies/providers
- lower socioeconomic status due to increased number of dependents in the home
- less supervision and structure
- greater risk of exposure to mentally ill family members
- lack of adequate training in disciplining and protecting the child.[17]

Increasing financial and community support for grandparents and family and friends' foster homes in terms of monetary and welfare assistance is likely to reduce the risk factors for the mental health of kinship foster children.

## Goals of foster parenting

To conclude this introductory chapter, here is a summary of the goals of foster parenting. The Child Welfare League of America (CWLA), the Annie Casey Family Foundation, the Dave Thomas Foundation, Foster Parenting International, and research from other organizations and countries have identified the following:[18]

- Provide a culturally sensitive approach to foster parenting.[19] For example, Singaporean children tend to have more internalizing behaviors.
- Protect and nurture the child (CWLA, Foster Parenting International).[20]
- Provide a network of support systems for the child.
- Be a professional team member able to work with the different aspects of the foster child's life.
- Provide detailed information that can help the providers and school identify developmental and academic delays.

Very importantly, work with the biological family to provide support, nurture that relationship, and ease the transition back for the foster child. This is the hardest, very frustrating, and most painful aspect as most foster parents will tell you.

It can leave you angry and hurt as well. Throughout the experience of foster parenting, it would be helpful to remind yourself that you are looking after this child for a short time, even if the time can be for over three years.

And remember, you are not alone when you feel frustrated. It is not always you, but the very challenging task you have taken on. Those in authority recognize your frustrations, so do not feel intimidated or afraid to voice your concerns.

## Notes

1. NSPCC 2012.
2. Child Welfare Information Gateway 2010a.
3. Modified from Broady *et al.* 2009
4. Tyebjee 2003; Peake and Townsend 2012; Cox *et al.* 2011.
5. Doelling and Johnson 1990; Buehler *et al.* 2006; Barth *et al.* 2006; Wilson 2006; Tarren-Sweeney *et al.* 2004; Peake and Townsend 2012; Koponen *et al.* 2009.
6. University of California 2008.
7. Child Welfare Information Gateway 2010b.
8. Rubin *et al.* 2007.
9. Preston *et al.* 2012.
10. Kjeldsen 2010; Wilson 2006.
11. Morrissette 1994.
12. Chen *et al.* 2011.
13. AARP 2006.
14. AARP 2013.
15. Smith and Boone 2006; Schwartz 2008.
16. AFPA 2006.
17. Annie E. Casey Foundation 2012.
18. Chipungu and Bent-Goodley 2004; Simmel 2007.
19. Woo *et al.* 2007.
20. CWLA n.d.

CHAPTER 2

# THE PLANNING STAGE

---

## About Your Family—Are You Prepared?

---

*"By failing to prepare, you are preparing to fail."*
—Benjamin Franklin

## Size of home

It goes without saying that all children need love and want to feel they belong. An important consideration, then, is to figure out if the number of children in the home is fewer than the home can handle. For example, if it is a three-bedroom home with two children sharing one room, a master bedroom, and a guest room, then there is space for another child or a same-sex sibling group.

In the USA, child welfare will not allow children of different genders to share a bedroom, unless they belong to the same family. By contrast, in the UK same-gender siblings can share a room only after a risk assessment is done. Therefore, the size and capacity of the home, and knowledge of the rules of child welfare in your region, needs to be the very first consideration when thinking about taking in a foster child.

## *Bedrooms*

A second consideration is the location of bedrooms. Common sense would dictate that bedrooms for special needs children would need to be on the main floor and near a bathroom if the child is physically disabled. It should be near the master bedroom if the child has to be closely monitored.

Some foster parents have used a bell over the door to notify them if a child is leaving a room. This is especially useful for potential sleepwalkers or children wandering into other bedrooms. Baby monitors are also helpful to track sounds and nightmares. Older teens prefer privacy but may also want to sneak out at night. With them, bedroom doors, front and back doors that have mechanisms to notify the parent if opened, or simple monitoring of the home is very helpful. Talking frankly and giving healthy freedoms to teens is also helpful.

## Your mental health

This is one issue that foster parents do not always consider when they want to take in someone else's child. Remember, this child is being 'loaned' to you for a period of time, and can just as easily be pulled out of your house with very little warning.

Are you prepared for the emotional and behavioral changes that you will experience? Think about trying to take care of a stranger; most of the time, you would expect them to be grateful. However, these children are resentful of losing their mother or father, and angry about being uprooted. If you foster a group of siblings, then it's "we need to stick up for each other, we're family" and it's them against you. Their anger and pain is then transferred to you, their foster parent. They lash out at you and try to hurt your feelings. Are you sure you are strong and mature enough to handle their pain?

Ask yourself, do you take things too personally? If they say they hate you, will your feelings be hurt? Might you get angry, or even abusive? Alternatively, would you be able to put it in perspective and recognize that they are talking about the rejection they feel?

Consider how you would feel about bonding with a child, and then having to deal with them moving on. Do you get attached easily? Do you have a supportive community that will help you cope with the sudden removal of your foster child whom you have grown to love?

Asking these questions at the outset is critical because they represent the challenges of foster parenting. Shockingly, there are five times as many incidences of actual abuse of children in foster care than in the general population. This does not mean that you are likely to abuse a child in your care, and it is not meant to discourage you from becoming a foster parent. It just means that you need to be aware of your own insecurities and have the capacity to seek help from family and friends.

Many times, biological parents do not show up for visitations when the children are eager to meet them. Many times, visitations get cancelled because a car breaks down, someone is sick, the supervisor cannot make it, the weather is very bad, the parents have not complied with drug tests, or the parents have failed the drug screens. All the above reasons are enough to put the child in a very bad mood and you have to deal with a moody, angry, depressed young person.

Can you handle your own anger about the parents' carelessness and lack of caring? How do you handle your own stress? Ask yourself difficult questions about your own behavior and personality.

If you have a good repertoire of coping skills in your life, you will be fine. Otherwise, shore up your defenses; you could be in for a rough ride. If you have a history of trauma, caring for a foster child may bring up traumatic memories that will affect you, and you may need to acknowledge your history. Be honest with yourself. Seek a good counselor for yourself and your own children to assist you in coping with this added stress. It is a very good idea to ensure that you do not introduce your own issues into your foster children's lives.

## Your children's mental health

A big issue that often is poorly dealt with is that of biological children in the home and older children who have left home but are concerned about their parents' welfare. A child placed into your home changes the family dynamics the moment they walk in. Critical issues that you need to ask and to reassure yourselves about before the child comes into your home include the following.

### How competitive are my own children?

If your children are competing with each other for your attention, they are going to be resentful of the addition of another child. If you have older teens, they are more likely to be tolerant of a very small child but unhappy with the younger kid who is constantly coming into their rooms or following them around.

### Does my child have to give up her/his space to accommodate another child? How should I handle it?

Talk to your child about making up for losing their space. Allow the child to participate in the decision-making process. What age would be comfortable for you? Would you be willing to share your room with a younger/older child? Talk openly about the ages/types of emotional or behavioral problems you would be willing to handle as a family. Children who have a say in the foster parenting process are more likely initially to accommodate a foster child.

## How will a foster child relate to me or my children?

When a foster child has lost her/his own home, the tendency is to treat the family as strangers, which they are. Depending on their relationship with their mother, they will fall into the role of a *rejecter*, *pleaser*, or *distancer*.

The *rejecters* tend to be in the most serious conflict with the biological children who have welcomed them and then bond with one child in particular who they look up to or share their confidences with.

The *pleasers* compete for love with the biological children and want the praise of the parent, and remain in jealous conflict with the biological children. This relationship works if the child is much younger and the older biological children then think she/he is "cute."

The *distancer* is accepted and ignored by the biological children and is allowed to have the space needed.

With humor, warmth, and tremendous patience, most relationship problems can be resolved. A healthy attitude for the entire family to have is to recognize early in the relationship that the children coming into your home are homeless, hurt and in pain, and are reacting in a normal way to a traumatic event in their lives. The new sibling group bonds together initially. However, once they get comfortable and the honeymoon period is over, the dysfunctional nature of the foster child's biological family may take over and maladaptive behaviors may start to appear.

## Ages and genders of foster children

When considering having a child placed in your home, let the foster agency know at the outset what ages and gender you are willing to foster, so that no unhealthy negativity develops in your relationship with the agency and the social worker.

Most sibling groups range from 16–17 years down to infancy. At the outset, your family needs to decide just how many children you are willing to take in. Sometimes it may be just one. Most of the time, children come in threes, but can be seven or eight siblings. Often the state workers will divide them into the girls or boys group, or younger and older groups so that the size is not overwhelming for foster parents. At any given time you may be asked to take in four siblings, ranging from five years old down to two years, and if the biological mother is pregnant you may also be asked to take in the newborn.

If you have young girls in your home, for example, it may be wise to foster younger children rather than older teen girls who have had street experiences with their biological mothers. Your daughters are very likely to emulate the older streetwise teenager despite your disapproval and a power conflict is likely to occur between you and the rebellious teen, as well as with your own children who will align with the foster teen.

**Table 2.1 Guidelines for ages and gender (safety-based)**

| Biological children | Preferred foster care children |
| --- | --- |
| Older teen boys and younger girls | Young girls and boys, older teen girls |
| Older teen girls and younger boys | Young girls and boys, older teen girls |
| Young girls and boys | Young children, or much older teen (>15) |
| Special needs infants | All ages above five years |

As a rule of thumb, it is not advisable to keep more than three children under the age of five years including your own, as parenting duties can be overwhelming.

## Choosing special needs children

Among the factors you will need to consider before taking in a special needs child are:

- availability of a supportive school environment with a special needs program
- financial resources
- respite care
- access to professionals—psychotherapy, speech and language, physicians, hospitals
- family and community support
- relationships with social workers.

## Buying clothes, shoes, room décor, and school supplies

Although this may seem contrary to common sense, often children in the foster care are bought clothing and shoes that differ from those of the biological children.

Foster parents need to be mindful of the fact that children in foster care feel they are a burden and there are those who feel a sense of righteousness because of the money the foster parent is being paid. We often hear children saying, "The state is giving her money to take care of me!" and the child feels cheated if the foster parents do not spend their funds on the child's clothing, activities, shoes, and so forth.

Resentment builds up, and anger and defiance are seen with passive aggressive behaviors such as refusing to clean their rooms, help around the house, or participate in family activities. The child will withdraw or in a desire to make a statement of their disapproval will do everything in their power to make you unhappy.

## Rules of the home

Rules that apply to your own biological children will need to apply to the children you foster to avoid resentment in your children.

Children who come from a home that has no rules or confusing enforcement of rules respond angrily at first, but with patience and determination those rules will be followed.

We as human beings have evolved from the animal kingdom and need to feel safe and protected. A house can be likened to a den, and rules to the rules of the wild. When children have clear rules and expectations they feel safe even though they complain. The foster child needs the following rules to be explained.

## Checklist of family rules and choices for consequences

- *What happens if I break something by accident?*
  Accidents happen.

- *What happens if I break something on purpose?*
  That may happen, but in real life every action has consequences. We will work together, figure out how to pay for it together, and you will not get hit, spanked, or hurt by me or anyone else in this family.

- *What are kids expected to do around the house?*
  You are family now and we all pitch in together. Let's see what you would like to do.

- *What areas am I not allowed to play in?*
  Give the same answer as for the rest of the children in the family in their age range.

- *What areas am I allowed to eat in?*
  Give the same answer as for the rest of the children in the family in their age range.

- *Up to what time can I use the phone?*
  Until shower/bedtime.

- *Do I have to ask to use the phone?*
  Yes/no/only before or after (state times)

- *Do I have to ask if I am hungry and want to open the refrigerator?*
  No! Many foster parents have this rule and some use padlocks on their refrigerators. This defeats the primary nurturing needs abused/neglected children have. They worry they will not have any food the next day, so want to eat more, or try to fill themselves with food as a way to take away the emptiness in their little hearts.

- *Can I have a snack before bedtime?*
  Choose healthy snack options.

- *What do I do if I am not hungry at dinner?*
  Do not force the child or punish her/him with no food.
  Let them eat later. Most are very hungry, but food is used
  as a control issue over a life they have no control over.
  Most foster kids will eat like there is no tomorrow, but
  some kids want autonomy or are too depressed, so give
  freedom of choice.

- *What if I wake up in the middle of the night and am hungry?*
  Come to me and I will fix you something. Don't be
  afraid to come to me.

- *Am I expected to hug everyone or only certain people in the
  house?*
  No! Foster kids choose people they connect to and foster
  mothers/dads need to hug them and hold them like
  small children. But, if sexual abuse is an issue, males in
  the house need to enforce boundaries and teach healthy
  touch/hugs and how to sit.

- *What is the best way to tell everyone to leave me alone?*
  Talk to me and I will tell the others. We can use notes
  on doors.

- *If I am not hungry, do I have to sit at the table?*
  Yes, we are family, and we need you too.

- *Can I watch TV if everyone is asleep?*
  If you have trouble sleeping I can help you.

- *Can I walk into rooms or do I have to knock?*
  Knocking is usually a good idea, as these children are
  fearful of the unexpected. So other family members
  need to generalize this rule. Also, privacy is important
  for teens and parents.

- *If friends of family come over, what do you expect of me?*
  Use the same rules you have for your other children.

- *If I cannot sleep what should I do?*
  Give the child choices such as "Wake me up," or "Ask me if you can watch TV."

- *What activities can I expect to be doing on the weekends?*
  Foster children need predictability and stability so give them a heads-up prior to each weekend well in advance.

- *How late can I sleep in on weekends?*
  Same as family.

- *Does your family go to church?*
  Yes (or no) and ask them which church or other place of worship their family attended.

- *Am I expected to visit relatives and what am I expected to call them?*
  Same as what your own children call them.

- *I have a boyfriend/girlfriend. Can I visit or call him/her?*
  Monitor closely.

- *What are the rules regarding inviting or calling girls/boys over the phone?*
  Monitor for sexual content. Let them know that your main concern is to protect them from harm and keep them safe.

- *What are the rules and expectations if I wet my bed?*
  No punishment, it's okay, you have been through so much, it's normal, we understand, just let me know and let's keep it between you and me, the other children do not need to know. Control liquid intake after 6pm.

- *Who should I go to when I have to confide something embarrassing?*
  Anyone you choose, but it should be a much older person. We just want you to be happy and safe.

- *What should I do or say when I am scared of someone in the family?*
  You can talk to me or _____. Your counselor, social worker, and I are responsible for your safety.

- *What kinds of actions/behaviors will get me into trouble?*
  Initially, we need to agree on those. How do you deal with anger? Sadness? Bad memories?

- *How are consequences decided and who gives me my consequences?*
  Only the adults and you will give you consequences. We can use a shoe box to write what consequences you get for behaviors, and you can pick any of them from the box. Whatever you pick is what you will get. It's up to you to choose your consequence. You get three choices. Pick the one you will do. (This gives power of choice to the child and prevents noncompliance.) Each consequence should have a time limit, and if it isn't done, the child has to also do one of the other two choices.

- *Add your own:*

  _____

  _____

  _____

  _____

All family members, including your children, need to meet and agree on the above questions and the answers you have decided. Keep these notes where every one of you can find them.

It will be helpful to a child who can read to then get a copy of the family rules so that there is no room for confusion. Any other family rules that are spoken and unspoken should be explained in a gentle and pleasant manner to the foster child, so that they understand what to expect. Most adjustment problems occur because foster parents who are new tend to address the above issues when and not before they happen, leading to unhappiness and resentment.

## Introduction to relatives

If there is one thing that makes a foster child cringe, it is being called a "foster child."

Experienced foster parents have the children call them "Granny," "Aunty," "Papa," a nickname, or even "Mama" to differentiate them from the biological mother. So, when the child is taken to visit relatives, the child is simply referred to as the relationship that was agreed upon. Relatives are then told not to talk about the biological family and warned not to gossip about the child's history. The more the child feels accepted by relatives, the more they are likely to accept your home and to follow your rules. A well-adjusted foster child is the goal.

It is suggested that social workers sit with each potential foster family, including their children, for a couple of hours to address these issues. Teasing out these minute but very critical issues will prevent endless frustrating moments that build up with your own spouses and children.

Just as children involved in difficult divorce and custody cases have a guardian *ad litem*, so also should every foster family have an in-home counselor designated to their particular family to address personal family adjustment issues, stress management techniques, marital relationship issues, relationship with biological children and biological parents, and family honesty regarding the range of problems they experience. Weekly sessions will be needed from the point of recruitment for these families.

# CHAPTER 3

# THE WELCOMING STAGE

## Getting to Know Your Foster Child

## Family history

Children enter the foster care system mainly because their parents are unable to take care of them adequately.

Their parents may have a mental illness such as bipolar disorder, schizophrenia, or major depression, and could be self-medicating with drugs such as cannabis (marijuana), crack, cocaine, heroin, or other drugs. They may also be overly self-medicating on pain medications such as Oxycontin or Vicodin, or on prescription medications such as Xanax.

Prescription drug abuse is quite common among teens, who may also sell them to others. It is important to know the background information about the child who is coming into your home so that you can be mentally prepared to handle the issues that child will most likely present. Therefore, as foster parents, you need to ask important questions regarding the child you are taking into your home.

## Questions you can ask about your foster child

- What is the child's full name?
- What does she/he like being called?
- Why were they removed from their mother/relative?
- At what age were they first removed?
- How many foster homes were they in previously?
- Why did they not work out for them?

- Do the children have telephone privileges and with whom?
- What are their eating, sleeping, and waking habits?
- Is the child a bedwetter? If so, how frequently? Does it worsen after visitation?
- Has the child been diagnosed with a mental illness/ mental handicap? If so, what is it?
- What medications and dosage is the child taking?
- When do I administer these medications?
- What effect does the medicine have on the child?
- Does the child have nightmares/night terrors?
- Does the child sleepwalk?
- Does the child have any odd habits/routines?
- What does the child do when she/he is angry?
- What does the social worker want me to do when the child acts out?
- Is the child afraid of anyone in her/his family?
- Who is the child's pediatrician?
- Does she/he have the medical card?
- What is the medical health of the child?
- What is the dental health of the child?
- What school should I enroll this child into?
- Is she/he in special education classes, and if so which ones?
- Was the child attending school?
- When are the visitations scheduled and how often?
- Who provides transportation for visitations and for therapy?
- Where does the child go for therapy?

- Which agency should I call regarding counseling in the home?
- Is the child being placed due to neglect, physical abuse, or sexual abuse, or some combination of the above?

## What you may not be told about your foster child

Some of the issues you may not be told about if you live in the United States include:

- the biological mother's and father's history
- sexual abuse history in the family
- placement of other siblings who are not placed with you
- other important relatives
- the condition of the home the children came from (details)
- how long you can expect to have the child
- why the children are being placed
- the specific reasons for moving the children.

## Behaviors commonly seen in foster children
### Behaviors due to neglect

These include:

- lack of knowledge about the three meals of the day
- hoarding food
- eating like there is no more food
- "stealing" from the refrigerator
- gulping down food
- bedwetting at night/day
- irregular bowel movement
- avoiding eye contact/staring into space

- hyperactivity, restlessness
- inability to sit still
- acting "wild" and out of control
- being scared
- refusing to accept blame
- seeming spaced out
- poor hygiene
- being fearful of shower/baths
- waking up at night to go to the pantry
- lying
- over-reaction to minor stressors
- clingy or withdrawn behaviors.

## Behaviors due to physical abuse

These include:

- whining
- shying away
- poor eye contact
- startled when touched
- aggressiveness towards others/self
- refusal to accept blame
- fear of being touched
- running away
- disrespectful/defiant behavior
- delinquency
- experimentation with illicit substances
- punishment has no effect
- unresponsive to threats
- refusal to respect authority

- tendency to lie even when observed doing something wrong
- suicidal ideation[1]
- self-harm.

### Behaviors due to sexual abuse

These include:

- punishment having no effect
- defiance
- anger and rage outbursts
- self destructive/suicidal
- cutting behaviors
- sexual acting-out behaviors
- lying
- stealing
- refusal to accept blame
- flirtatious behaviors with strangers
- easily going to strangers/fearful of strangers
- disruptive
- inattentive/stares into space
- fearful of the dark
- nightmares/night terrors
- not having body boundaries
- running away
- lesbian/gay experimentation.

## To work or not to work?

Foster children need extra time, attention, and care due to their lack of control over their lives.

An important consideration, then, is to juggle work demands and childcare demands so that you are available emotionally and physically for your child. Patience, time management, maternal sensitivity,[2] and responsiveness are critical for these children, and you want to take into consideration your realistic capacity to handle work demands while raising foster care children. Two-parent homes are more likely to be able to meet these demands, as are single mothers/fathers of older children. Studies have shown that two-thirds of foster mothers work full-time as foster parents. In the UK, 40 percent of the foster parents cited monetary compensation as helpful in terms of motives to remain foster parents.[3] Those who work outside their home use childcare for their biological and foster children.[4]

## Schools

It is strongly recommended that for ease of transition from one school to another, every foster child should immediately access the local school no matter when they join, be tested right away for academic level, be placed with same-age peers and taught specifically at that level, be provided with specialized tutoring for subjects they are clearly weak in, and have their education tailored to their needs.

Along the same lines of European countries, North American countries should also have a "surrogate educational mentor" to follow the child's education all the way to graduation and college/work entry. Policy decisions will need to be put in place to enforce implementation of these changes. This is especially important as clinical experience has shown that 50 percent of children in foster care are diagnosed with some form of Special Education Needs (SEN).

Below, I have provided some guidance in relation to school placements. It is beyond the scope of this book to provide an equally detailed account for countries outside of the USA, so I have instead provided a list of useful addresses where the reader can find up-to-date guidance relating to their particular area.

## Academic placement in the USA

According to a recent study completed by the Casey Family Programs, 64 percent of children in the US foster care system are school-age and are 2.5–3.5 times more likely to be enrolled in special needs education.[5] American students have access to Individualized Educational Programs (IEPs) and you as a foster parent can ask for one.

Previous school placement, academic levels, and the child's adjustment are factors that schools take into consideration when placing your foster child. Usually, the new school will not have any records, and these children miss many days of school before they are first placed. As a result, unless you have children functioning within their school grade/school year, their grades can be expected to be lower than other children of the same age, and they will need emotional support through this difficult and frustrating academic adjustment period.

If you live in certain states such as California, AVID (Advancement Via Individualized Determination) is a program that connects middle-schoolers in foster care to college readiness; and in Hawaii a "surrogate" is appointed to take care of the foster child's academic needs throughout their school education. If you do not have access to these programs, ask for school testing (IEP),[6] especially over the summer before school starts, or after the first month of school so that the child does not get increasingly frustrated and lose motivation. Other countries have a mentor, or an "authority," appointed by the commissioner/local authority to oversee each child's education as this is compulsory and heavily emphasized.

You may find it useful to browse the Legal Center for Foster Care and Education (www.americanbar.org/groups/child_law/ what_we_do/projects/education.html) for an overview of some of the issues.

## Academic placement outside of the USA

For readers in other countries, here is a list of useful websites to fostering organizations well placed to offer advice specific to your region.

### UK
*England*
The Fostering Network, England
www.fostering.net/england

*Scotland*
The Fostering Network, Scotland
www.fostering.net/scotland

*Wales*
The Fostering Network, Wales
www.fostering.net/wales

*Northern Ireland*
The Fostering Network, Northern Ireland
www.fostering.net/northern-ireland

### Australia
The Australian Foster Care Association
www.fostercare.org.au

## Notes

1. UK statistics: children aged 11–17 had six times higher suicidal ideation and self-harm as compared with non-abused children (NSPCC 2011).
2. Ponciano 2010; Roque and Veríssimo 2011; Van Den Dries *et al.* 2012.
3. Peake and Townsend 2012.
4. Smith *et al.* 2001; Buehler *et al.* 2006.
5. National Working Group on Foster Care and Education 2011.
6. Tubbs 2002.

# CHAPTER 4

# THE DISPLACEMENT TRAUMA STAGE

## Understanding Your Foster Child

Children in foster care are uprooted from their biological homes at any time of the day or night, and I call this "displacement trauma," which may revisit these children during their sleep at night.

To many of these children, being taken away from their caregivers—however inadequate—represents a displacement of their set view of their world and day-to-day expectations. Chaos is one such expectation, and routine can seem frightening and confusing at first.

It is to be expected, then, that children will often describe their worst experience as: "I got taken away from my mom." This is perhaps the most frequent response I have had from children in placement. It does not matter that they may not have seen their mother for days, or weeks, or, as one state worker shared, that they lived in an "infested home with no food, no stove, and dirty clothes, did not go to school, purplish bruises on child…" or that they were beaten by their mother's boyfriend; it's all a part of being with Mom. Maybe she will change.

Foster parents entering into a contract with a foster child have to harmonize their role as the foster parent with the child's perception of Mom or Dad. They choose to take in a child, but the child has no choice when they enter the system. As a result of this inequity, the child then demonstrates a set of behaviors that the foster parents see and hear. The parent then categorizes the child mentally as perhaps a cooperative or a defiant child. Successful foster parents are those who, through experience and instinct, learn to "empower" the child so that she/he learns to become self-reliant and confident.

Some of these children often resist adjusting to foster care, pine for the absent parent, and are defiant, oppositional, aggressive, withdrawn, or just simply guarded. They enter into therapy, often complete psychological and psychiatric evaluations, and may be on medications. These are the *rejecters*.

Then there are those children who are so grateful to be removed that they never want to go back. They are the *pleasers*, the ones who wait to serve their foster parent and to be loved. At first, after they get adopted, the guilt, self-loathing, and shame set in and the dynamics of unresolved attachment and abandonment surface. They act out and turn against themselves in their pain.

Many children have very strong loyalties to their families and refuse to bond to the foster family. Or, as in most cases, they have moved from one foster home to another and maintain a comfortable and safe distance from the foster family, following rules but lacking in affectionate gestures, words, or actions. These are the *distancers*. They go through life making superficial and meaningless connections with those who they come into contact with. They use people for what they can give them and then discard them just as perfunctorily.

There are still other children who are so relieved to have been removed that they immerse themselves in their foster home, openly and willingly look up to their foster parents, and are delighted to be "home." Adoption is pure joy, the end to the endless confusion and fear of returning home, and fear of losing their new home. They never wish to leave and once adopted settle down in their behaviors and grow up to be resilient and happy youngsters. These are the *changers*. They change the family dynamics.

So, which category will your foster child fall into? Within a group of siblings who are fostered, or "sibship" as they are called, each child may fit into one of the above categories. You will not necessarily have all of the resistant rejecter child, the pleaser, the distancer, or the changer: the oldest child in the sibship is generally the parental figure for the others who will then closely watch her/his behaviors and follow.

Sibling groups tend to be formed in the following way. The oldest child may be the pleaser delighted to be finally rescued from the terribly abusive lifestyle. Or, he/she may be the rejecter and act out so much that they disrupt the foster home placement for the younger siblings. Loyalty to the biological parent is a powerful force for this young person, the "head of the household" now that the parents are no longer living with them. This child then encourages, subtly to be sure, the younger ones not to listen, not to follow directions; and ultimately, in frustration, you as the tired foster parent turn to the social worker and tell them this child has to go. This is an all too common situation that plays out over and over again.

So, here we have our rejecter absolutely refusing to be a part of your family and being defiant, argumentative, and seeming to be purposely trying to make you lose control. Rejecters need to be handled differently from children in the other categories. They need to feel in charge of their lives and be allowed to be loyal to their biological parent. The goal here is to make the child believe that you are on their side and on the side of healing their wounded parent. Once you succeed in convincing this child that you will do everything you can to help their parent, this child will turn into your assistant and help you! It seems very simple, but the power of filial loyalty and the power of a mother should never be underestimated.

The pleasers worry me the most. They are sweet and gentle and very obedient as young children. But wait till they get older. Suddenly this child can become defiant, sneaky, and shock you with actions you never thought they were capable of. This is not because the child has had a personality change. Rather, it is due to the child's deep-seated resentments surfacing, and as they feel secure their brains are now willing to process their unresolved trauma. So you see the sudden emotional outbursts of crying uncontrollably, the acting-out behaviors, perhaps being very secretive and withdrawn. All of these behaviors can be handled if you do not react to them with shock or anger. Stay calm and let the child know that you are willing to give them whatever time they need to regroup and let the child know they are still loved very much. Firmness and punishment will destroy years of hard work you have put into this child. You will be viewed as "the enemy."

The distancer is the one that will have multiple placements, just as the rejecter will. But, in this case, the rejecter is sabotaging the placement before you abandon him/her.

The changers are our most resilient foster kids and need no explanation. They overcome the odds, thrive in adverse situations, and push themselves to succeed. As one young woman wrote to me yesterday, "I lived by the book and finished college." Yet another one went on to join the navy. Many foster children are the first in their families to enter college or have a well-paying job.

---

## Question: How would you describe the foster children in your care?

As you go through this resource guide, ask yourself which type of child you have, and as you turn the pages, find behaviors and emotions typical of your child and learn how to handle them.

---

# THE ADAPTING STAGE

## Attachment and Protecting Your Foster Child

From a psychological point of view, successful placements for foster children depend on the foster parent, the child, and the interaction between the two.

Successful placements have the following qualities:

- Children want to stay in the foster home.
- Children have more positive social behaviors.
- Children feel that their foster parent is responsive to their needs.
- Children feel loved and accepted for who they are.
- Children feel that their foster parent responds to their needs.
- Children are placed with their siblings.
- Children have control over their depression.

> **Question: Does your foster child have any of the above qualities?**

## Adapting to infants (0–5 years)

Infants up to the age of two years learn three basic life skills from the mother/child bond. These are:

1. trust
2. cause and effect thinking

3. identifying and tuning into others' emotional states.

These basic life skills lead to:

1. increased sociability
2. greater compliance
3. good control over emotions.

Secure children demonstrate the above skills, while children with insecure attachments tend to develop emotional and behavioral disorders, also known as EBD. EBD children are two-and-a-half times more likely to have four or more placement changes than non-EBD children.[1] So how can we create more stable children within foster care? What else can be done? The answers lie in developing a bond/secure attachment with your foster child.

Both new and existing foster parents are equally capable of forming secure attachments with their foster care infant.

## Attachment/bonding issues

Often the words attachment and bonding are heard during parenting classes and skills training workshops. But what do they really mean? To understand this concept from a foster parenting view, consider the following.

There are two basic kinds of attachment. These are:

1. secure attachment
2. insecure attachment (seen in physical abuse, severely deprived infants).

Both of these are based on the dyadic relationship (parent/child) between the caregiver and the infant.

In *secure attachment*, infants are able to communicate their emotions and use their caregiver as the person they want to stay near. From that person, they explore their environment. In foster care, approximately two out of ten infants have secure attachment and are likely to be fairly easy to love and nurture.

There are three types of insecure attachments. Two of those are called organized insecure attachment: they are *avoidant attachment* and *resistant attachment*. In avoidant attachment, infants do not interact with the caregiver and show very little negative emotion under stress. In resistant attachment, infants show intense negative emotions with the caregiver and want contact but cannot settle down after a separation from the caregiver.

The third type of insecure attachment is *disorganized attachment*. In this type of insecure attachment, the infant shows fear of the caregiver, freezes, cannot be comforted by the caregiver in times of distress, has stereotypical movements, and seems to have no direction that she/he is headed towards when caregivers approach them. Studies[2] have shown that as many as 80 percent of severely deprived infants have disorganized attachment. Caregivers who show threatening or frightening behaviors have disorganizedly attached infants. Table 5.1 summarizes the types of attachment.

In the United States, 67 percent[3] of most mother/child attachments are secure attachments, 21 percent avoidant, and 12 percent ambivalent/resistant in the general population.

**Table 5.1 What to expect: types of attachment and foster parenting[4]**

| | |
|---|---|
| Secure attachment | 0–70% of infants; pre-adoptive, sensitive mother |
| Insecure attachment | Less sensitive foster mother, non-adoptive |
| Avoidant | 10% of infants in foster care; 33% adolescent mothers |
| Resistant | 9% of infants |
| Disorganized | 22% of infants; 33% adolescent mothers |

## Developing secure attachment in your new foster infant/child

Numerous studies[5] have identified two main ways of establishing secure attachment with infants/small children. These are:

1.  *Show maternal sensitivity.* Sensitive mothers are described as being able to recognize the needs of the infant and the meanings of different behaviors. More sensitive foster mothers have more securely attached foster infants even if they have worked and have childcare.

2.  *Show maternal responsiveness.* Correctly interpret the infant's signals, including negative emotions. Respond to the infant's signals correctly. A lack of this recognition leads to avoidant attachment, and inconsistent responding leads to disorganized attachment. Fathers can emulate these traits when Mother is absent to create a bond.

A Chinese study found that children who were once in foster care, rather than in an institution, showed better emotional and behavioral regulation post-adoption over time. This was an international adoption study done on 92 children, 50 of whom were adopted from institutions, and 42 of whom were adopted from foster-care placements.[6] There have been studies done elsewhere with similar results. This shows the positive effects of foster care.

## Behaviors seen in infants and small children

To assist you in developing maternal sensitivity and responsiveness, here are some facts about foster infants and children to keep in mind:

*   Infants need emotional security and protection to survive.
*   Early experiences have long-term effects on mental and physical health.

- By the end of their first year, infants learn what to expect from caregiver, self, others.

- Disorganized attachment is a strong predictor of later childhood behavior problems.

- Foster care children have trouble with the way they express emotions.

- Infants and children give behavioral messages that are confusing.

- Infants and children do not know how to ask for affection.

- Children are torn between emotional bonding with parents/foster parents.

- Foster infants and children act as if they do not care to be loved or need you.

- Foster infants and children expect to be rejected.

- Foster infants and children tend to walk without eye contact and with their head averted from you.

- With biological parents they may fling their hands in front of their faces [a stress reaction] or appear frightened.

- Foster infants and children can make you feel rejected even when they want your nurturing and love.

- Foster infants and children do not know how to control negative emotions.

- Foster infants and children do not know how to show positive emotions appropriately.

- Foster infants and children do not understand negative emotions.

- Foster infants and children show more negative emotions.

- Foster infants and children are more sensitive to aggressive actions.

- Foster infants and children over-react to minor stressors, and can shut down for no obvious reasons.

*Remember:* Due to attachment problems with their biological mother/caregiver, foster infants and children can often appear to be distant, uncaring, indifferent, disobedient, "driven by a motor," do head-banging, pull hair, have sleep and eating problems, have intense emotions, and be difficult to soothe. Rocking the child, holding, putting words to their facial expressions of anger and fear in a calm relaxed soothing voice, singing, cooing, tucking into bed…these work to calm them down.

## Attachment and its impact on visitation

Due to anger, grief, and resentment, biological parents can appear cold and angry during the visitation, while the infant/child can be clingy, tearful, or rejecting of the biological parent.

Night terrors, nightmares, crying spells, acting-out behaviors, and occasional bedwetting can also be expected. Instead of asking to reduce those visits and worsen the attachment problems, you as foster parents need to hold and care for the child after these visits to reduce the long-term effect of separation from the child's mother. After a visitation, the strong emotions that accompany attachment disruption will show themselves in the child's emotions and behaviors. Gradually, with increased visitation times and days, the child will bond better with you and be happier during and after visitation.

## Helping the child to gain emotional control

Table 5.2 shows useful techniques to help the infant or small child to develop control over their emotions (emotional regulation) so that their behaviors and reactions can be controlled. There are ways to work around the problems of insecure attachment and its negative effects.

**Table 5.2 Techniques for helping the infant/small child to control their emotions**

| Behavior taught | Result |
| --- | --- |
| Teach the infant/small child to persist in a task. The motto is: "Try, try, and try again until you succeed." Don't allow the child to give up | Suppressing attention problems |
| Delay gratification with reinforcement | Child learns to control emotions |
| Turn-taking | Child learns to control negative behaviors |
| Show how you handle frustration: smile and say it's okay when they make a mistake | Calming the infant's/toddler's fears |
| Model behaviors that show emotional control | Child learns to control intense emotions such as disappointment |
| Model appropriate ways of showing sadness and disappointment | Child learns it's okay to show sadness and disappointment |
| Take the child to the mirror and show positive faces—smiling, laughing | Child learns to identify and show positive emotions |
| Show consistency in discipline and use a calm tone of voice and manner | Child is mentally prepared and accepting of consequences |
| Show negative emotions appropriately | Child mirrors and accepts negative emotions |
| Name emotions for the child | Child learns to name feelings |
| Express anger without aggression | Child learns anger is a safe emotion |
| Hug, hug, hug and cradle the infant, hold and rock the child, even an older child—they need enormous amounts of love | Child learns not to fear physical contact |

## Mental disorders and behaviors as a result of attachment problems

These typically include the following:

- reactive attachment disorder
- conduct disorders
- night terrors
- bedwetting
- inconsolable crying
- hoarding
- picky eating
- nightmares
- fear
- anger.

### Reactive attachment disorder

As stated previously, infants up to the age of two years learn three basic life skills. These are:

1. trust
2. cause and effect thinking
3. identifying and tuning into others' emotional states.

Abused infants do not learn the three basic life skills. As a result, they develop emotional and behavioral problems.

### Conduct disorders

Conduct disorders in children in foster care are caused by:

- insecure attachment
- hostile parenting:
  - coercion
  - verbal aggression
  - physical aggression
  - harsh discipline

- mother's history of depression.

Consistent discipline with love works for dealing with conduct disorders. You can tell the child: "You are the only one responsible for your actions. No one else is. It is your behavior that is the problem, not you; you are an amazing child who can (name skills). I want you to teach me how you (name something good)! I want to see more of that from you."

Human beings tend to live up to others' expectations, so if you brand the child as being "just bad" the child will work to fulfill that prophecy. Patience, training, involvement in positive feedback, and self-esteem enhancing activities reduce those behaviors over time. Increasing attachment also reduces those behaviors. Simply rewarding the child with material goods or praise will not work after some time and the expectation will always be to be bribed to be good.

## Adapting to older children and adolescents (6–16 years)

Older children and adolescents are greatly influenced by the parents and caregivers they left behind. Their views about adults are well formed and they will transfer these opinions to you, their surrogate parent. They may have obvious behaviors such as aggressive acting-out behaviors, or they may have less obvious behaviors such as very high anxiety, depression, and fearfulness. In the following sections, the dynamics of aggressive behaviors and anxiety are discussed.

### Anger and aggression

- Why are my foster children so angry and aggressive?
- What skills need to be taught?
- How can I teach them these skills?

*Why are my foster children so angry and aggressive?*

Older children and teens can show aggressive behaviors due to their childhood history of being exposed to aggression. Aggressive behaviors are known to be transferred from one generation to the next and show by the time the child is eight years old. If left unchecked and kept in the dysfunctional home, these children grow into aggressive, hostile, and violent parents.

This is why children who are physically abused or exposed to domestic violence have a higher risk of returning as adolescents and young adults into the legal and juvenile system for delinquency.

There are three forms of exposure that can lead to aggressive behaviors in preschoolers, older children, and teens. These are:

1. A harsh parenting environment: physical abuse, domestic violence, uncontrolled anger and aggression.
2. Absence of emotional control, and impulsiveness on the part of the parent.
3. Unemotional and neglectful parent(s): lack of guilt and empathy.

Angry and aggressive young children have been known to grow into violent and aggressive teens if inadequate or no intervention is made.

Perhaps the easiest way to talk about aggression is by explaining the different types of aggressive behaviors. Once we understand these differences, we can then work on handling their outcomes.

PROACTIVE AGGRESSION

Here the child attacks another person without any provocation. Studies have shown that children who have proactive aggression:

- are less rejected by their peers
- do not react strongly to provocation
- lack guilt and empathy

- show poor response to punishment even if reward is offered
- have neglectful, rejecting, and unemotional parents
- have low fearfulness
- have low capacity to inhibit their behaviors.

### REACTIVE AGGRESSION

Here the child reacts to a real or imagined threat to their body. Numerous studies have shown that these children:

- are rejected by peers
- misjudge the hostile intent of the other person
- have low frustration tolerance
- have a history of forceful and abusive parenting
- have low control over their emotions.

It needs to be stressed that aggressive behaviors that are first seen in preschoolers will continue into childhood and teen years if no intervention is made.

## What skills can I teach them?

### LACK OF EMPATHY

To develop empathy, children will need to receive training in moral development. In children, moral development generally begins around the age of seven years. Prior to that, children learn right from wrong based on whether they are punished for their actions or not. In dysfunctional homes, children can be punished for refusing to steal or refusing to commit acts that they simply feel uncomfortable doing. They learn that it is right to steal and wrong to refuse. They have no sense of guilt for their actions because, in their mind, they did the right thing. Moral retraining is needed for these children to expose them to society's view of right and wrong. This causes great confusion and anger, and upsets children to the point that they have nightmares, bedwetting, and proactive aggressive acting-out behaviors.

Your task as a foster parent will be to develop and enforce morality training.

## CASE STUDY

Joe and his foster mother came in for a psychological evaluation. Joe was stealing, not listening, cried when he had to get up for school, was eating all the time, had poor hygiene, lied about taking showers, would not answer any questions, was hitting other foster children and picking on them, and breaking things. Then he often looked right at the parent, shrugged his shoulders, and denied doing any of those things. Now he was no longer talking to anyone. In frustration, his foster parent gave the case manager a 14-day removal notice and a consultation was needed. During the clinical interview, Joe disclosed that his mother made him steal from the neighbor's mailboxes, was high on cocaine most of the day, and told him that school was only for kids whose mothers did not love them and sent them away to school. He hung out with much older boys in the neighborhood, ate from garbage cans, helped his mother by counting her cigarettes, and brought her drugs as well when she sent him for them. His mother rewarded him by giving him a dollar to buy candy. That was his moral development until the age of ten years. This was what he knew as his reality.

### What works

Let the child know that his mother does love him very much but was not herself due to the drug abuse. Let him know that she wanted what was best for him. Put down the biological mother and you will lose the child!

LACK OF CONTROL OVER THEIR BEHAVIORS

Angry acting-out behaviors are learned by children from their parents, based on:

- observation of the parent's behaviors
- continued interactions with the hostile, angry, and aggressive parent.

Removing these two powerful maintaining factors from their environment leads to reducing this memory trace and opening up the child to new ways of reacting to stress.

### LACK OF CONTROL OVER THEIR EMOTIONS

As in infants and children under five years, the same behaviors can be modeled, demonstrated, and validated by foster parents of older children and teens in order to develop emotional control in their foster children. Your own older children need after-school activities that keep them busy, but younger children tend to learn from their siblings and can try to imitate foster children.

### POOR PEER RELATIONSHIPS

Research has shown that children aged over 11 years in foster care tend to have more placements, more problems with peer relationships, and difficulties with social skills. They can be mean, be bullies, be bullied, want to fit in with well-liked peers, and turn to dysfunctional peers for approval and acceptance. Girls in foster care are at higher risk of multiple placements due to a lack of sense of belonging. At times, the defiance and distrust of adults leads to greater bonding with other peers, and in their desire for love and nurturing they can become victims of abusive boyfriends. Showing your pre-teen positive ways of respecting herself and others, teaching cues about behaviors, and modeling positive interactions by older foster children helps younger children learn appropriate ways of handling conflict. Teen girls are often involved with controlling, abusive boyfriends, having seen their mothers being treated the same way. Teaching self-respect by showing her how her boyfriend is abusive, that it is not right, and how she should be treated as a young lady helps her increase her self-esteem and make better choices.

### LOW FRUSTRATION TOLERANCE

Anger against a biological parent, negative thoughts and emotions, and lack of a sense of being whole lead to a low level of frustration tolerance in foster care children. Increasing frustration tolerance will require delaying gratification for increasing amounts of time, for example waiting for a minute, gradually increasing that time to five and ten minutes, etc. until it is an entire day.

### EXPECTING BODILY HARM FROM PEERS

Due to their history of physical abuse and their view of their world as being hostile, children in foster care have a stronger sensitivity to their bodies and feel vulnerable and easy prey for victimization. It is therefore important to teach them ways to respect their bodies and to protect themselves. A simple way to handle these fears is to let the child approach you first, then allow you to hold her or him, and then allow you to hug her or him with permission. Increasing healthy physical contacts reduces hostile acts.

### POOR RESPONSE TO PUNISHMENT

Physically and sexually abused children are poor responders to punishment. Grounding, taking away privileges, yelling, spanking...none of these methods work. What works is talking and nurturing, anticipating behaviors, and increasing expectations; treating the child as a thinking, feeling little person with a right to their views; a lot of respect (even when you don't think they deserve it); and an outstretched hand of unconditional friendship and agreement on the rules.

### What else works?

Provide healthy lifestyle choices and children will blossom and grow. Allow numerous mistakes and errors of judgment. Remember that you are dealing with a child who has a very warped sense of reality by now. Acting-out behaviors such as screaming, hitting, kicking, fighting, cursing, very poor table manners, extremely poor hygiene, and fear of water are not uncommon due to the extreme fear of a new and unknown lifestyle. Humor, joined laughter, kindness, and gentle and diplomatic handling of these sensitive issues will be needed.

*How can I teach them these skills?*

To develop these skills in the angry and hostile foster child, the foster parent needs to show the following parenting behaviors:

- Show supportive, calm, non-aggressive, and empathic parenting.
- Model non-aggressive social behaviors.
- Demonstrate conflict resolution techniques in hostile situations.
- Show a capacity to allow the child to show anger without retaliating with rejecting behaviors.
- Allow each child to express anger, disappointment, and rage in socially acceptable ways.
- Define behaviors that are acceptable and not acceptable by wording them as "safe" and "dangerous" to the child. Each time, the foster parent will need to stress that the goal is to protect the child from herself/himself.

## Anxiety

- Why are foster children so anxious?
- How can my foster child become less anxious?
- How can I reduce their anxieties?

Children who are removed from their biological homes often suffer from anxiety and distress following their removal. They are now living in a stranger's home, with new and strange surroundings, new rules, a new set of "foster" siblings, and new relationships with the members of the foster family. They react with an initial honeymoon period of withdrawal and compliance. These children are anxious because they are preoccupied with when and how they can go back home.

*Changes in anxiety and types of anxiety over the years*

Anxiety is a normal reaction of the human brain to perception of an outside threat. There are two basic types of anxiety:

1. transient
2. persistent.

According to Dr. Daniel Pine from the National Institute of Health, *transient anxiety* can be short-term (lasting for hours or a number of days), or medium-term (lasting for a number of days or weeks, up to a month). *Persistent anxiety* lasts for months or even years and has serious long-term mental-health consequences.[7] With foster children, the repeated uncertainties in their lives lead to higher levels of anxiety than normal and can become persistent. This is probably the reason why young adults transitioning out of foster care experience higher than usual levels of panic disorder, sleep disturbance and are seven times more likely to self-medicate (using illegal drugs) to try to alleviate anxiety than the general population.

*Age-related changes in anxiety for children in foster care*

- *18 months to 3–4 years.* Separation anxiety.

- *4–8 years.* Imaginary and reality-based fears of monsters, flying insects, Chucky (a villainous fictional movie character), scary movies, school-related fears, scary characters in windows, fear of mother being killed in traumatic ways, fear of never seeing mother again.

- *9–18 years.* Failure, reality-based fear of physical injury, school-related fears, fear of abusive parent, fear of never seeing mother again, fear of mother being dead, fear of never finding mother again.

Young children often do not know that they can dream of something they wish they had. To them, dreams are generally fearful nightmares.

*Signs of anxiety in foster care children*
These include:

- restlessness
- fidgeting
- staring into space
- defiance
- crying for no reason
- sweating
- night sweats
- bedwetting
- soiling clothes
- cowering
- irritability
- sleep problems
- difficulty falling asleep
- difficulty staying asleep
- waking up several times during the night
- sleepwalking
- feeling very tired after a night's sleep
- stomach aches
- headaches
- overeating
- picky and finicky eating.

*Types of anxiety disorders commonly seen in foster care*
(*Caution:* This section is not meant to help you diagnose your child, but to help you understand her/his diagnosis.)

As a foster parent, be prepared to take your foster child to a therapist, psychiatrist, or psychologist. Terms will be used that may not always make sense or that you may not agree with. Here is a list of anxiety disorders that you will hear:

- *Acute stress disorder.* In this diagnosis a child experiences a traumatic event that has resulted in extreme fearful reactions and lasts from anywhere between two weeks and four months. The child may show symptoms of sleep problems, irritability, restlessness, and watchfulness towards adults.

- *Panic disorder.* Typically, this is an illness in which the body is over-aroused, with symptoms of faster heart rate, choking sensation, feelings of dread, tingling sensations in fingers and hands, and dry mouth. It can occur with fear of small spaces or of closed spaces, or without that particular fear.

- *Generalized anxiety disorder.* In this disorder, there are six months of off-and-on symptoms of sweating palms, edginess, feeling something bad is about to happen, excessive tiredness, spacey behaviors, and sleep and irritability problems.

- *Obsessive compulsive disorder.* Children who are molested or fearful of judgment tend to be very compulsive about their surroundings. In my clinical work I have talked to sexually abused children who will especially ensure that their belongings are kept in certain order and arrangements, and some will even wake up at night and redo their entire closet. They need to have security through predictability. Typically, OCD has symptoms of repeated thoughts or actions which cause distress to the child. They know something is wrong, are very upset about their symptoms, and are generally secretive about them. Children who are removed due to severe physical abuse are terrified of the abuser and will get up and check the doors and windows and make sure that all of them are locked and bolted. That is not OCD but a compulsive trait or behavior that is due to trauma.

- *Post-traumatic stress disorder.* PTSD is perhaps the most commonly diagnosed disorder in children in foster care.

This diagnosis has key features of exposure to intense traumatic experience(s), intense reactions that include flashbacks, a sense of unreality, a numbing of emotions so that they seem to talk about the events as if they do not bother them, exaggerated physical and emotional responses, rage reactions at times, and a fight or flight response to what they see as being dangerous.

### Ways to help the anxious child or teen

- Keep routines simple and easy to follow.
- Listen to the child and provide eye contact, a willingness to accept what the child is experiencing.
- Allow the child to experience positive life events—birthday parties, family time, activities—that are fun and relaxing.
- Do not attach value to failures.
- Convert negative events to learning experiences.
- Teach the child to laugh at themselves and their errors and to accept themselves.
- Teach relaxation/breathing techniques.
- Have something to look forward to each day.

## Depression

Often anxiety is a precursor to depression. Depression leads to problems in several behavioral and emotional areas. The following behaviors are typical of foster care children:

- school under-achievement
- refusal to adjust into the foster home
- sadness
- crying spells
- stealing
- fighting with other kids

- hurting self (cutting, pulling out hair)
- refusal to eat
- hoarding behaviors
- staying in their room
- refusing to socialize
- impulsively reacting
- defiance
- screaming
- pouting/sulking
- hitting
- wiping feces on walls, tables, etc.
- sibling and other jealousies
- suicidal gestures, threats, and attempts.

## Types of depression

Depression can be short-lived and temporary when children are removed from their biological caregiver, or it can be longer and more permanent and then it is diagnosed as a disorder. During the adjustment period, children can experience depression about the sudden and unclear changes in their young lives. They can react by withdrawing for the next few days, weeks, or months, and unless nurtured, welcomed, accepted, and loved, they can sink into a deeper depression. The sorrow of their own biological mother's inability to care for them is expressed differently in children compared with adults.

Children may show external acting-out behaviors with mean acts towards other foster children, picking on younger peers, hitting, biting, screaming, and fighting. Or, they may show what we call behaviors that are internal acting-out behaviors such as not talking, silence, refusing to look directly at others, not paying attention, sleep problems, eating problems, and bowel and bladder problems such as bedwetting.

## Types of depression seen in children in foster care

There are two primary types of depression. *Endogenous depression* is genetic and *adjustment disorders* are environmental. Some depressive disorders can be both genetic and environmentally caused.

Children in foster care are most commonly diagnosed with:

- *Adjustment disorder with depressed mood.* Generally, this diagnosis is given to foster care children who have just been placed and have been experiencing symptoms of depression for at least six months.

- *Dysthymic disorder.* This diagnosis is given to children who have experienced depressive symptoms for at least two years. Their impairment can be mild, moderate, or severe.

- *Major depression.* This diagnosis is given to children who suffer from depression that is more severe than occasional blues, and instead is persistent and impairs the child's functioning in significant ways.

- *Bipolar depression.* This diagnosis is given to children who are often whiny and moody, have difficulty differentiating reality from fantasy, and often view themselves and the world negatively at times or can be agitated, irritable, and have grand unrealistic views of themselves at other times. These children have mood swings, make false allegations against their foster family and peers, and can act like they are the victims of abuse that may not have occurred.

## Parenting your child with depression

- Identify the problem. Talk about what makes the child sad, how she/he feels, and make a list.

- Encourage the child to keep a journal.

- Encourage the child to talk to one adult member of the family or an older teen.

- Help the child identify feelings. Children can misinterpret sadness for anger and then feel disappointed in themselves.

- Identify goals that the child can work towards.
- Improve self-esteem by watching for positive behaviors.
- Compliment positive behaviors and kindness in the child.
- Give the child special parent/child time.
- Provide structure and routine to keep the child occupied.
- Do not allow the child to stay in their room alone for more than an hour or so.
- Encourage outings with family members.
- Encourage the child to explore new behaviors that are healthy.
- Encourage after-school activities such as drama, wrestling, or swimming.
- Assist the child with developing coping cards about how to cope.
- Show the child how to process her/his depressive thinking with the help of a counselor.

Children in foster care show far more anxiety and depression than children who live with fairly well-adjusted biological families.

Disciplining techniques that worked wonders with your own children will not work with foster care children. They will hoard food, hide in closets, tear clothes, destroy objects, break things on purpose, chew on their clothing, bite their nails, hurt themselves or others, bully or get bullied… All of these are due to severe problems of neglect and/or abuse.

## Notes

1. Barth *et al.* 2005.
2. Smyke *et al.* 2010; Van Den Dries *et al.* 2012.
3. Van IJzendoorn and Sagi 1999.
4. Van Den Dries *et al.* 2012; Ponciano 2010; Bernier and Dozier 2003.
5. Jee *et al.* 2010; Albers *et al.* 2010; Van Den Dries *et al.* 2012; Chamberlain *et al.* 2008.
6. Van Den Dries *et al.* 2012.
7. Pine 2012.

# CHAPTER 6

# THE EDUCATIONAL STAGE

## Parenting Issues and Much More

*"Wisdom is not the product of schooling but the lifelong attempt to acquire it."*

—Albert Einstein

*"Anyone who has never made a mistake has never tried anything new."*

—Albert Einstein

## Intra-family coping issues

Despite all the training prior to first getting your foster child, the behaviors that subsequently surface can be very trying and taxing on the existing family system.

Foster children can be difficult to manage and love because of the multiple negative experiences they have had to learn to cope with in the past. Such experiences leave scars on their young formative minds and they react in ways that foster parents find difficult to understand. As a result, you may suddenly feel inadequate, and question your own capacity to love this stranger unconditionally and to always be forgiving. It is very tempting at this stage of foster parenting to throw in the towel and to simply give up. So how can you deal with your own anger and feelings of being rejected? And how can you remain emotionally stable in the face of so many failures?

This is the stage where the agency worker, providers, and foster parent training step in to provide the additional support to the foster parent. Placement disruption is a risk at this point. Foster parent retention is the critical task for the agency at this juncture.

Agencies and support groups can encourage foster parents to stay in six major ways:

1. Improve the foster parent's skills training.
2. Create open communication channels between foster child, parent, and worker.
3. Provide sensitivity training with regard to the child's history and behaviors.
4. Provide frequent communication and feedback, phone calls, and venting sessions.
5. Provide family counseling via the in-home therapist.
6. Address the child's reasons for her/his behaviors and work on strengthening the foster parent/child relationship.

## 1. Improve foster parent's skills

While there are many ways to intervene at this stage, the most important skills are:

- Learn that the child's behavioral reactions are a result of their families of origin.
- Learn to connect to your child by demonstrating safe and nurturing behaviors.
- Learn what works with regard to discipline and why.
- Learn how to adapt effectively to the child's intense emotions.
- Learn how to establish safe and firm boundaries between the child and others.
- Learn to accurately anticipate the child's reactions to most common situations.
- Learn to provide safety in those situations so that the child learns how to gain self-control.

## 2. Create open communication channels

- Verbalize emotions in a healthy pro-social manner.
- Do not use words like "always" or "never."
- Say "It makes me feel…" rather than "You are acting…"
- Do not use blame or shame.
- Do not threaten removal of the child (the child will expect it).
- Let the child know you are strong enough to handle their pain.
- Let the child know you are not rejecting them, but want changes in behavior.
- Speak with calmness, kindness, and patience.
- Provide multiple opportunities for success.

## 3. Provide sensitivity training for foster parents

Earlier we noted that successful foster parents demonstrate maternal sensitivity.[1] This means:

- Recognizing of the child's negative and positive emotions.
- Recognizing that the child is unable to control the intensity of their emotions.
- Recognizing that the child over- or under-reacts to normal stress.
- Being aware that the child's signals for communication are not the same as for "normal" children.
- Being aware that the child comes to your home with low self-esteem, hopelessness, developmental delays, grief over separation from their biological family, anger, and resentment towards adults.
- Being aware that the child is confused, lost, and often does not know what is right or wrong, and even if she/ he does, refuses to accept responsibility for their actions.

- Being aware that the child fears retribution and expects the foster parent to be punitive and unpredictable.

## 4. Provide frequent communication and feedback, phone calls, and venting sessions

- Be available when the foster parent calls you for help.
- Answer phone calls within the hour during work hours.
- Identify a back-up state worker for the families to call.
- Have a list of resources that the families can turn to in times of crisis.
- Provide prompt feedback in response to questions about particular behaviors or needs, or requests for supplies.

## 5. Provide family counseling within the foster home

A normal period of adjustment to a new life situation is generally defined as a six-month period. In foster children, due to their attachment issues and delays, it can be much longer. Foster parents will need supportive in-home intervention until that adjustment period is complete, during and after visitations, and after court dates and important changes such as medication and starting school. You as the foster parent can use the counselor as a sounding board for disciplining issues, to understand the child's behaviors, to learn how to cope with changes, and to understand your foster child better.

There are different specialized therapies that are available specifically for treating neglected and abused children. While these are available in the United States they may not be available in other countries. The programs available there will be provided at the end of this section.

Specific evidence-based parenting and trauma treatment programs that can help you parent your traumatized child are:

- Attachment therapy.
- Functional family therapy.
- Attachment and Biobehavioral Catch-up (ABC) Intervention.
- Development Education for Families (DEF).

You may wish to ask your therapist or counselor for more details regarding the above-mentioned therapies. Since the ATTACh program has received wide attention and is more easily understood, this therapy is discussed further below.

### Attachment therapy

Although the other three programs are just as important, we focus here on a 12-component treatment program called the "Treatment, Theory, Protocols and Strategies for Children and Families with Attachment and Bonding Problems" program, based on attachment therapy techniques endorsed by the Association for Treatment and Training in the Attachment of Children (ATTACh). The goal of attachment therapy is to repair and provide a corrective experience to early negative life experiences. This is done by teaching techniques such as nurturing parenting behaviors and providing sensory motor experiences that give the child a sense of safety and comfort.[2]

## 6. Work on strengthening the foster parent/foster child relationship

Children are torn between wanting to accept their foster parent and feeling that if they do so, they are rejecting their biological parent. They struggle with these emotions and can become moody, rude, and difficult. To this end:

- The child should feel comfortable with addressing their foster mother as Ms., Mom, or Grandma, or any other term that is appropriate for their relationship.

- Explain to the child that they are in no way choosing to love one parent over another.

- Explain that they are here for as long as the courts will allow them to stay.

- Explain that when their parents are ready to take them back, you will assist them with the transition.

- Explain that until such time, there are rules that they need to follow so that their stay is comfortable and they can be happier.

- Explain to the child that by doing well, they will make their parents proud and teachers will comment on their positive progress. They will be able to focus on themselves and their future. This will lessen the worry for their biological parents.

- With young children, often what works is when the counselor and foster parent tell the child that the courts and workers are assisting their parents so that they can have a clean and safe house to go back to. Children are generally willing to accept this if they have some sense of time frame. In cases of substance-abusing parents this cannot be said. The lack of consistency is a frequent source of disruption. This is perhaps why studies have found that children from homes with substance abuse histories tend to have anywhere between five and nine placements during their childhood and adolescence.

## School-oriented issues

### Special education needs for foster children

Due to the nature of why these children entered foster care, educational assessments are often required. Many of these children have been neglected and have not attended school regularly. They may have stayed home. Their mother/caregiver could have moved them several times over the years and school admissions would have been disregarded. Older children could have been staying home to care for their younger siblings.

When these children come to your foster home, their academic levels are unclear. Often they struggle with reading and writing and are unresponsive when asked to read. They are too embarrassed to let you know that they cannot read or write.

That is the main reason why in the United States, Individualized Educational Programs are recommended for newly placed children, unless they have actually been attending school previously and their grades are known.

For purposes of their school assessment, the child should complete at the very least an IQ test and an academic achievement test in school. Based on the child's IQ and academic levels, the child will receive specialized services. Also, if the child has behavior problems in school, there are criteria based on which the child will be placed in an ED (emotionally disturbed) or MH (mental handicap) classroom or a classroom setting that provides appropriate accommodations for their special needs.

### What is IQ and what does it mean?

IQ, or Intelligence Quotient, is a range of two numbers within which the child is functioning.

| IQ | Range |
| --- | --- |
| Average IQ | 85–110 |
| Borderline | 70–84 |
| Low average | 84–90/95 |
| High average | 100–110 |
| Above average | 110–124 |
| Very superior | 125–160 |

| Level of mental retardation | Range |
| --- | --- |
| Mild | 55–70 |
| Moderate | 40–55 |
| Severe | 15–40 |
| Profound | Below 15 |

## Learning disabilities

The criteria for the diagnosis of learning disabilities require an average IQ with problems in reading, spelling, writing, and/or mathematics. Again, schools and clinical psychologists will be able to test children for the specific learning disabilities they might have.

## Special needs children

In the United Kingdom, the system differs depending on which part of the UK the child lives in. Children are placed in nursery, primary, and secondary education within the public school system. Each of the four nations has separate laws regarding this critical aspect of foster care, so those readers outside of the USA who want more information about the law and education systems specific to them can refer to the links at the end of Chapter 3.

*UK*
*England*
The Fostering Network, England
www.fostering.net/england

*Scotland*
The Fostering Network, Scotland
www.fostering.net/scotland

*Wales*
The Fostering Network, Wales
www.fostering.net/wales

*Northern Ireland*
The Fostering Network, Northern Ireland
www.fostering.net/northern-ireland

*Australia*
The Australian Foster Care Association
www.fostercare.org.au

# Mental health issues

Studies have found that anywhere between 50 and 80 percent of children in foster care have mental health diagnoses and as young adults,[3] and young children are diagnosed over 2.5 times higher than the general population.[4] Familiarize yourself with these major diagnoses that children in foster care are most often diagnosed with.

## Reactive attachment disorder (RAD)

RAD is unique to foster-care children, and is frequently misdiagnosed as bipolar disorder. That is why it is explained in detail here. RAD is caused by insecure parent/child attachment. Due to the lack of consistency of love, and hostile and angry actions by the caregiver towards the infant, the child develops pathological attachments with new caregivers. The DSM-IV 1994[5] describes two subtypes of the disorder:

- *Disinhibited type.* Overly friendly, goes to everyone, hugs and kisses indiscriminately, moves very easily from one caregiver to another.

- *Inhibited type.* Refuses to bond with caregiver, distant, seemingly uncaring, and very suspicious of motives of others.

RAD usually begins in the first year of life and certainly before the age of five and is due to pathogenic care (neglect, abuse).

## Typical RAD child reactions

RAD child reactions are typically fear of harm, tenseness, anger, manipulative, charming, friendly, preoccupied with violence, distrustful, cannot show emotions, blank expression, cannot give love, or gives too much love.

Outcome behaviors are:

- *Inhibited.* Refusal to be touched, shies away, stays in room, poor eye contact, coldness, distancing, refuses to hug, refuses to bond, suspicious, cold, controlling, destructive of property, cruel to others, makes up obvious lies, lies even while knowing they have been caught in the act, steals, impaired moral development.

- *Disinhibited.* Overly friendly, calls everyone Mom or Dad, hugs, kisses, pushes themself on others, wants to be hugged, talkative and warm to complete strangers, wants to go home with your friends, asks very personal questions of strangers, lies even while knowing they have been caught in the act, steals, no conscience.

## Parenting skills specific to your RAD child

You as foster parents have many opportunities to develop bonding with your foster children. These are:

- Modeling positive social behaviors.
- Creating a nurturing environment, providing:
  ○ safety
  ○ care
  ○ support
  ○ warmth.

- Emotional coaching to develop empathy by teaching about emotions and how they affect us and others.

- Engaging in social, personal, family interactions with the foster child. Name the emotions the child is feeling. For example, if the child looks angry after losing, you can say, "You look like you are really mad." When the child denies it, make a comical imitation of the facial expression without looking directly at the child, and usually children will smile or laugh or sulk some more. Walk up to a mirror and show the child your angry face and ask them to look in the mirror as well. When the child eventually starts talking, provide meaning for the anger and appropriate expression of the anger. You have just prevented a meltdown or angry aggressive reaction towards a peer or another adult. With consistency of feedback and role playing, children become more aware of their own emotions and recognize their triggers for anger, anxiety, sadness, and so forth.

- Swaddling and cuddling the child. Smaller children can be wrapped snugly in their comforters, surrounded by teddy bears and other soft cuddly animals with half-closed eyes. Large open eyes even on snuggly animals can be very frightening at night.

- Imagination time. Sitting by their beds at night and reading a happy fairy tale is wonderful. Let them use their imagination and make up the story as you go along. This develops emotional regulation and also helps prevent nightmares and night terrors. Start with "Once upon a time..." and add enriching and positive experiences to bad situations. Teenage girls also respond well to this sleep routine. Their brains do the rest during their dreams. By doing this, you are rewiring their brains and teaching them new accommodation skills so that now they will handle their insecurities and emotional problems differently. If you have more children of different ages, adjust their bedtimes so that you can do the same with the other children.

- Hold and rock the child often. When small children and even teenagers are in distress, picking them or letting them sit on your lap and holding and cuddling them can be very comforting. Even with sexually abused girls, as long as this is a female foster parent. With boys, foster mothers can pick them up and hug them. You can let them sit next to you and put your arms around them and let them know they are safe (if the boys have sexual arousal this would be inappropriate).

## Attention deficit/hyperactivity disorder (ADHD)

Not all overactive behaviors are due to ADHD. Emotional control problems lead to hyperactivity. Drug and alcohol exposure can also cause overactivity and lack of control over their behaviors.

ADHD, which occurs because of lack of adequate stimulation to the brain, is a biochemical disorder, and has a genetic basis. In the United States, preschoolers are diagnosed with ADHD 40 percent more often than in other countries, perhaps partly because of the heightened awareness of ADHD amongst teachers in the United States. It occurs four to five times more often in boys than girls.

As a result, the brain searches for stimulation and the child appears easily distracted, inattentive, and hyperactive. A common myth is that the child is overstimulated and acts out; however, the opposite is true. Once adequately stimulated, the child can focus and stay calm. Stimulants are therefore prescribed.

True ADHD consists of a complex of 18 core symptoms. However, children without control over their emotions and behaviors can also mimic signs and symptoms of ADHD to the point that studies have shown that 50–60 percent of children diagnosed with ADHD are misdiagnosed. To be diagnosed with ADHD, a child should have these symptoms in at least three different settings, have symptoms at the age of six or earlier, and measure significantly higher on psychological objective tests for ADHD.

The DSM-IV lists three major types of ADHD. These are:

- *Inattentive type.* Poor attention to tasks, distracted, forgetful, clumsy, forgets instructions, needs instructions to be repeated, and cannot concentrate.
- *Hyperactive/impulsive type.* Will not sit still, moves constantly, fidgety, restless, blurts out answers, impatient, cannot wait turn, fights, poor social relationships.
- *Combined type.* A combination of the inattentive and hyperactive/impulsive types.

## Typical child reactions

- *Poor emotional regulation.* Child whines, difficulty with problem solving, shuts down.
- *Emotional reactions.* Complains mildly, complains loudly.
- *Outcome behaviors.* Sulks, pouts, pushes, hits, yells, screams, fights, refuses to follow directions, violates rules, disruptive, defiant, pushes, teases, curses, runs away, threatening behaviors.

## How to treat ADHD

- Medication. Research shows that behavioral management with low-dose medications are the most effective in long-term functioning.
- Development of cues for social skills.
- Academic tutoring.
- Behavior modification techniques. Calendars, teaching self-control, talking while writing the next step of an action all decrease impulsive acts.
- Neuro-biofeedback.
- Nutritional changes.

## Parenting skills specific to ADHD children

Of all the ways one can intervene, researchers have found that there are four key areas of successful interventions in ADHD:

- *Situational advice.* For example, assist the child with specific help with challenging tasks (e.g., teach the impulsive child to put toothpaste on the brush without messing up the countertop, show how to pour milk without spilling).

- *Warmth.* This critical dimension is showing affection, pride, nurturing, love, care, kindness, and encouragement.

- *Structuring the task.* For example, help with homework instructions, break it down into easy steps, and assist with completion in stages.

- *Responsiveness to child's distress.* This goes back to our discussion of maternal sensitivity towards the child's emotional state. Allow the child to express anger, irritation, and frustration and validate their emotions. Scolding the child for cursing, yelling, or throwing will not only alienate the child but weaken your bond. Instead be observant to the early signs of frustration and intervene immediately to prevent escalation of the distress.

## Unsuccessful parenting skills

- *Showing negative emotions.* Looking frustrated, acting annoyed, irritated, angry, saying words with a negative tone.

- *Intrusiveness/control.* Taking over the task just to get it done with.

- *Withdrawal.* Turning your back on the child and doing something else, not helping the child in any way, looking disinterested.

### Parent's own self-regulation skills

- *Parent's anxiety/distress.* Degree to which you can control your own anxieties, preoccupations, or helplessness when the child is distressed.

- *Parent's overall self-regulation.* Ability to balance being calm, relaxed, and interested in the child's activity with managing your own emotions appropriately.

### How to adapt to your ADHD child

- Provide clear structure with the same daily routine; create a daily checklist.

- Put a checklist (and pen) in the bathroom to be followed when they wake up. Have the child check off each item as it is done.

- Give the child medication before school (most ADHD medications need 20 minutes to take effect).

- After school, ensure that the homework assignments are done when they come home, and observe for ADHD symptoms. An afternoon dose may be needed.

- Maintain close dialogue with teacher regarding missed assignments.

- Structure homework times and schedules.

- Observe if the medication effect is wearing off. These are the ways to know:

  o The child is losing focus and whiling away time during homework.

  o The child takes too long to complete a problem or sentence.

  o The child seems hyperactive or easily distracted.

  o The child skips problems or words while reading.

  o The child is picking on everyone else.

- Have a bedtime routine that begins at least half an hour before bed. Gradual transitions are needed.

- Give one instruction at a time and wait for the child to follow it.

The key to successful parenting of ADHD children is to interpret situations correctly, develop an awareness of their own focus on the negative aspects of their lives that they cannot control, and teach appropriate ways of letting you and others know they are experiencing emotional distress.

## Fetal alcohol spectrum disorders (FASD)

About one child in a thousand born in North America has a history of prenatal alcohol exposure, but these children are over-represented in the foster care system to the extent that 80 percent of them are then placed in foster care by age 12. Maternal poverty and substance abuse are the main contributing factors with 1.4 percent of pregnant women admitting to binge drinking during their pregnancies. FASD is found in 1 percent of infants born in the United States.[6]

Fetal alcohol spectrum disorders include the following:

- fetal alcohol syndrome (FAS)
- partial FAS (pFAS)
- fetal alcohol effects (FAE)
- alcohol-related neurodevelopmental disability (ARND)
- alcohol-related birth defects (ARBD).

These disorders are caused by the mother's exposure to alcohol while carrying her unborn baby. There are many neuro-developmental delays as a result. Unlike ADHD, which can be due to genetics, or RAD which is caused once the baby is born, FASD is in-vitro environmentally caused. The impact is permanent but the degree of disability can vary from mild to severe.

*Typical primary child symptoms of FASD*
These include:

- poor short-term memory
- speech and language delays
- poor judgment and problem-solving abilities; learning disabilities
- problems understanding cause/effect relationships
- problems in generalizing information, abstract reasoning skills
- planning and organizing impairments
- impulsivity
- fairly severe social and emotional problems
- inability to read social cues
- lack of boundaries
- difficulties understanding, reading, and expressing emotions
- poor sense of concept of time
- difficulty with sensory cues of hunger, pain, and temperature.

### Typical secondary effects that can be prevented/reduced
These include:
- dropping out of school
- alcohol and drug related problems
- inability to live independently after reaching adulthood; homelessness
- heavy dependency and lack of direction as young teens and adults; victimization.

### Common issues relating to FASD parents
These associated issues will often lead to placement breakdowns:
- *Insufficient knowledge and information.* Did not know about the FASD diagnosis, lack of information about FASD,

viewed as bad parents, did not know what was wrong with the child.

- *Fear of harm to family.* The child is violent at times, foster parents cannot go anywhere, fear for safety sometimes, the child maltreats others.
- *Conduct problems.* The child is aggressive, dangerous to self, repeatedly runs away, hygiene and health problems.
- *Child is not adapting.* Cannot keep up with routines, seems like every instruction is new, does not seem to retain anything.
- *Exhaustion.* The child develops an unhealthy attachment to their foster parent, too big to handle, burnout, too much work, tried everything, nothing works.
- *Taken for granted.* Not enough support, not enough agency understanding of the problems, blaming foster parents for not bonding.

These issues can be overcome, but foster parents who are more resilient, and likely to continue to foster FASD children, include those with:

- personal or family experiences with alcohol
- concern for the chronic needs of the child
- previous parenting experiences and realistic expectations.

### Parenting strategies specifically for FASD children

These include:

- using memory aids such as post-it notes, calendars, notes on the bathroom mirror, agenda for appointments
- using self-talk during transition times from one activity to another
- personal time-out from exhausting routines
- forced separation from child/respite care

- talking to friends, partners, and older children, and enlisting their help
- setting boundaries repeatedly for the child in terms of body space and behaviors
- focusing on the child's positive behaviors
- writing down every detail that needs to be done and delegating responsibilities to each person.

## Oppositional defiant disorders (ODD)

Often children with ADHD may also have ODD. These children have frequent negative, hostile, defiant, and disobedient behaviors and attitudes towards authority figures. Children with ODD who are more likely to have later emotional and behavioral problems are the ones who also show irritable and headstrong behaviors early in life.

Specialized parenting programs are used for noncompliant children, such as "Helping the Noncompliant Child: Family-Based Treatment for Oppositional Behavior." Other techniques that have been helpful in managing ODD are collaborative problem-solving (CPS) techniques or Barkley's parenting training (PT), which can be taught to you and your family by your therapist.

### Typical child symptoms of ODD
These include:

- frequent temper tantrums
- excessive arguing with adults
- often questioning rules
- active defiance and refusal to comply with adult requests and rules
- deliberate attempts to annoy or upset people
- blaming others for his or her mistakes or misbehavior

- often being touchy or easily annoyed by others
- frequent anger and resentment
- mean and hateful talking when upset
- spiteful attitude and revenge seeking.[7]

*Parenting strategies that work with ODD children*
- Learn about the causes of ODD.
- Use a daily school-home report card.
- Learn positive attending skills.
- Work with therapist to develop a contingency plan.
- Learn how to use time-out effectively.
- Watch videos on dealing with ODD.
- Learn how to diffuse conflict.
- Anticipate negativistic behaviors.
- Have structured family routines each day.

*Goals for parenting ODD children*
These include:
- building necessary interpersonal skills
- building self-esteem
- developing empathy
- developing morality
- developing vulnerability.

## Obsessive compulsive disorder (OCD)

Although this is actually an anxiety disorder, it is addressed here due to the number of children in foster care who show this particular disorder. OCD symptoms are seen more in children with histories of trauma. Those who have had to deal with terror and violence are fearful of being kidnapped, have strange thoughts that repeat themselves in their minds and cause great anxiety and distress, and seem preoccupied, distant, and inattentive.

Actually, they are intensely afraid and try to take away the bad thoughts by actions that may seem strange to you. They will often check to see if the doors are locked and the windows are closed tight, repeat certain words in sequence over and over in their heads to prevent something bad from happening, and a real giveaway with these children is when you see them do a certain series of actions as a ritual every single time! It could be what they eat in the morning every day, how they put their clothes on, or how they react when the sequence changes. Often, these children are mistaken as autistic due to the strict way they need to follow their rules, but it is really because they feel if they break their ritual something terrible is going to happen to someone they love, usually their mother or siblings. They seem to doubt everything you ask them because in reality they are not sure themselves and question with "What if?"

The most common symptom is hoarding. Foster care children are compulsive in that they will take every candy, candy wrapper, and food they can find in the house and hoard it. They may hoard it under their pillow, under their mattress, in the closets, baskets, toy chests...anywhere they find places to hoard food.

Self-injurious behaviors such as picking at scabs, scratching, hitting themselves, chewing on themselves, or biting themselves are common.

School can be challenging because they have to be "perfect" and they can write so slowly that it can be very frustrating. Or, they will refuse to write, because they do not like the way they write.

Symptoms of OCD are often seen in children who have been sexually abused. The child will need a counselor. At home, walking around the home with the child, letting them see that they are safe every day, making the child feel that you are powerful adults who can actually protect her/him, will go a long way to making them feel safer.

## Serious sexual behavior problems

In the United States, epidemiological studies have shown that one in four to five girls and one in six to ten boys is molested, depending on the criteria of the study. In the UK, statistics are that one in four children are molested before they turn 18.

Some children show no signs while others are very sexual and are unable to control their sexual impulses.

### Typical child reactions

These include:

- sudden and unpredictable rage reactions
- over-reacting to changes in schedule
- does not like unpredictable situations
- acting out when feeling unsafe
- manipulating, lying, stealing
- poor body boundaries—pushes him/herself into the adult
- has a lot of interest in male and female sexual parts
- tries to make sexual comments, acts out sexually
- sneaky and dishonest
- running away behaviors as a teen
- cannot trust
- cutting, hurting self
- needs to be the one in control otherwise turns defiant and oppositional.

### Parenting strategies that work with sexually abused children

- Educate yourself with the help of the counselor about normal sexual development, attachment problems, safety planning, and sexualized behaviors.
- Make the child feel they are in control of their life.

- Don't use punishment. It does not work. Use your listening and attending skills.

- Use creative tasks to develop your relationship, such as sand play, molding clay, making necklaces with beads, drawing, painting, doing your nails together, and brushing hair. With boys, try clay modeling, putting together car models, and hands-on activities that empower their sense of nurturing and strength; for example, gardening, planting flowers, growing plants/ trees, taking care of animals, and taking leadership responsibilities. These hobbies develop empathy and give them an outlet for their negative energies of fear and anger. Praise, encouragement, kindness, and affection work very well with these children.

- Don't close the door when you enter their room.

- Ask for permission before you enter their room.

- Be respectful, kind, and polite even when they are rude or defiant.

- Give them space when they ask for it.

- Let them know you understand they do not trust you.

- Do not probe their history. They will tell you when they are ready.

- Watch your own body language.

- Keep your tone neutral during conversations.

- Don't try to form a bond. Wait for the child to approach you first.

- Be honest and frank about your lack of knowledge of what the child is experiencing.

- Show willingness to be vulnerable to your own issues.

- Protect your other children from possible sexual exploration.

- Keep a bell or other form of warning to let you know if anyone is entering the child's room at night or the child is leaving the room.
- Accept that the child is trying to manipulate you often and calmly work around it.
- Inform the child well in advance where you are going.
- If the child is going out, know where the child will be going.
- Teach breathing and self-calming words to conquer panic attacks, cope with fright, and handle stressful situations.

## Pervasive developmental disorders (PDD)

Pervasive developmental disorders include autism spectrum disorders (ASD), childhood integration disorder, and Rett syndrome.

Of these, autism spectrum disorder is the best known and includes both autism and Asperger's syndrome. Autism begins before the age of 30 months. It includes difficulties with bonding to the biological mother; problems with communication, social smiling, and interacting; and the need for routines which, if disrupted, cause great distress to the child.

### Typical behaviors of a child with ASD

These include:

- avoids eye contact
- does not smile back at you
- does not know how to play with toys
- does the same series of movements over and over again
- walks on toes
- plays alone; not interested in others

- aligns objects in order and certain sequences
- follows a set of routines
- seems independent for age
- will not follow directions and seems hard of hearing
- enjoys sounds in the left ear such as music
- tends to rock back and forth or side to side
- carries out stereotypic movements such as repeatedly doing the same action
- has trouble expressing needs
- may wave their hands or arms to show happiness or joy
- may hit themselves to show sadness
- may run from you for no reason
- can be self-injurious or hyperactive.

*Parenting strategies that work with ASD children*

- Become very involved in the child's life.
- Go to the school regularly.
- Follow at home the same routine that the child does at school—for example, putting up coat, taking off shoes, sitting at table.
- Keep a behavior journal.
- At the dining table select two behaviors you want to teach or reinforce each week, and let the child earn bright colorful stars for eye contact or eating with a fork/spoon, and show the child it's great to show positive emotions such as laughter.
- Keep a behavior record and use resources in the community.
- Ask for help from your counselor regarding shopping trips.

- Routines are critical. Teach words for transition from one task to another and give plenty of time to transition with reminders about the transition said repeatedly.

- Join a specialized training program for foster parents.

- Children with ASD love color. Use it generously to reward them.

- Maintain routines always, but introduce slight changes gradually to encourage new behaviors.

- Children with ASD have certain talents. Encourage the talent into a hobby.

- They are good on computers so encourage them to write and play games.

- If an intellectual disability is also present, as in autistic children, work on simple communication skills and activities.

## Speech and language delays

Speech and language delays are commonly seen in children in the foster care system. Specific behaviors include screaming, head banging, pouting, hitting. As speech improves, the negative behaviors decrease. The goal is to learn to interpret what the child is trying to say, and to teach alternative ways of expressing their frustrations. Play therapy is remarkably useful to express feelings. You can also ask to have increased speech therapy and train yourself with the help of the therapist.

## Delinquency and substance abuse disorders

Children with early emotional and behavioral problems may develop delinquent behaviors six years later, according to some studies. To prevent delinquency and substance abuse, specialized parenting programs are available and very successful, such as the Incredible Years Intervention Program for parents of children 3–11 years old. Details are provided in the next chapter.

## Genetic disorders

Fragile X syndrome is a diagnosis given to children with an X-linked dominant genetic disorder. These children usually have learning problems, unstable moods, and can be diagnosed with mild to severe intellectual disabilities and autism.[8] Physical limitations, eating problems, and sensory deficit problems can be expected with children with celiac disease. Physical limitations and aches and pains are complaints of children with sickle cell disease. Mild to moderate mental retardation is often found in children born with Down's syndrome. Difficulty holding objects, problems walking and holding themselves upright, and grip control problems are found in children who are born with cerebral palsy.

## Cocaine babies

Children who are born with cocaine in their systems have multiple learning disabilities in reading and mathematics. These infants cry more easily and are difficult to soothe. Unlike normal infants, distracting the cocaine infant worsens the crying because of the change caused by introducing new objects. They develop ADHD symptoms and learning disabilities. ADHD medication that use stimulants such as Ritalin do not have any effect on cocaine babies later in life. Solutions that have proven effective include a highly structured classroom setting, simple stepwise instructions to children, and smaller classes.

Parenting strategies include:

- *Do not overstimulate the infant/child.* Keep their schedules simple, predictable, and limited to a few activities.

- *Light touching.* Cocaine infants dislike being touched but need it. Diaper changes and clothing changes need to be done quickly and efficiently with minimal touching.

- *Patience is the key.* Cocaine withdrawal takes anywhere from one month to four or five months. The infant will remain difficult to soothe, cry a lot, and need moderate stimulation.

# Family issues

## *Coping with schedules and time constraints*

Due to the number of biological and foster children, time management is a strength in foster parenting. If you have good time management skills, you are likely to still be challenged by the many unpredictable events that can occur while foster parenting. For example, the school can call and request a change of clothes when the foster child has an "accident," that is, soiling or urinating on them.

Children could be in different schools depending whether they are attending elementary, middle, or high school. You will need to schedule pick-ups and drop-offs, arrange for childcare, and identify back-up emergency resources. Your case manager will be most helpful in this regard and can assist you with organizational issues.

## *Time management*

Foster parents who are successful have learned to clearly designate chores with clear expectations to their biological and foster care children. Charts regarding chores, activities, schedules for school, visitations, counseling, and agency-related activities are easily accessible and visible. Children who are from abusive homes do not do well with unpredictable day-to-day changes and need routines that are mostly the same every single school day.

## *Dividing attention with biological and foster care children*

Successful foster placements have been those in which the biological children feel they are a part of the rescue/caring for the displaced foster children. Their parents reported increased empathy, kindness, and caring in their own children as a result of this experience.

## Personal issues

It is important to remember the axiom "Take care of yourself before you take care of anyone else." Take time for yourself: intimacy, personal space, re-grouping energies, friendships, and work.

## Relationship issues

Collaborate with peers, teachers, providers, biological family, and community the child belongs to.

## Agency-related issues

Develop collaboration with agency staff, court mandates, and providers.

## Notes

1. Ponciano 2010; Chamberlain *et al.* 2008; Van Den Dries *et al.* 2012.
2. www.attach.org
3. Pecora *et al.* 2005.
4. Clausen *et al.* 1998.
5. APA (American Psychiatric Association) 2005.
6. Centers for Disease Control and Prevention 2012.
7. American Academy of Child and Adolescent Psychiatry 2009.
8. Garber, Visootsak and Warren 2008.

CHAPTER 7

# THE EMPOWERING STAGE

## Successful Evidence-Based Strategies

Children enter into the foster care system with problems in the areas of parent/child relationships, delays in their development, lack of nurturing, and inconsistent parenting, and many were forced to parent themselves. They lack a whole sense of self or a sense of others. This emotional damage is then placed on the foster parents into whose home they enter. As foster parents, you will be entrusted by the state to meet these children's basic needs and emotional needs, and to undo the damage done to them by their biological families.

The single most important factor in empowering you as foster parents is to practice "caring" behaviors.

## Basic needs of all children

All children need:

- food
- safety
- to feel loved
- to feel secure/protected.

The goal of successful foster parenting is to provide a caring environment in which all of the above basic needs are met. As foster parents, you will need to meet additional psychological needs. These are:

- Create positive bonds with other members of the family.
- Provide constant caring and nurturing of the child.
- Show multiple ways of giving positive affirmations by noticing and approving:
  - small acts of kindness
  - acts of caring on the part of the child
  - acts of helping
  - empathic behaviors
  - healthy affection.
- Develop simple rituals, for example child/parent special time, meal time.
- Model expressing positive feelings and actions.
- Model expressing anger and sadness.

## Steps in empowering foster parents

### 1. Self-assessment

In caring for foster children, the first step is self-assessment. Self-assessment involves assessing parenting skills in terms of (a) parenting strengths and weaknesses, (b) personal strengths, and (c) personal vulnerabilities. Write down and identify the following areas.

*Parenting strengths*
These include:

- establishing boundaries
- setting limits clearly
- dividing attention between children
- being flexible with behavioral issues
- listening to children.

*Parenting weaknesses*

These include:

- inability to handle arguments
- tendency to take things personally
- problems with knowledge of stages of development
- lack of knowledge of the challenges of parenting traumatized children
- lack of knowledge of community resources to help parent your child.

*Personal strengths*

These include:

- stability of own emotions
- self-awareness
- self-satisfaction
- satisfying relationships
- positive view of self
- enjoy own company
- like yourself
- healthy self-esteem.

*Personal vulnerabilities*

These include:

- needing approval from others to feel good
- feeling you are lacking in happiness
- need for comfort often
- wanting others to be around most of the time
- isolation needs
- lack of self-respect
- absence of sense of internal comfort

- unable to tolerate disagreements—foster parents who are inflexible are likely to have severely acting-out foster children.

The Children's Workforce Development Council (UK) has set parenting standards for foster parents. These include self-development and understanding your role as a foster parent.

## 2. Evaluating domains of empowerment

Empowerment from a parental perspective is the degree to which you feel you can raise your foster child effectively. To do so, examine your relationship with the child in the following areas.

*Competence*
Areas to examine include:
- adequate child development knowledge
- range of child management skills
- feeling reinforced by the child's positive responses
- acceptance by the child's social worker
- praise/support by the child's social worker
- understanding of your role and limits as a foster parent
- not taking everything the child says personally: foster parenting is about learning about the child's experiences.

How to increase your sense of competence:
- Attend foster parent education classes.
- Join a foster parent discussion group.
- Get emotional support from the group.
- Have your efforts validated by the group/agency personnel.
- Develop a file of resources—these could be family resources, community resources, parenting programs.

- Gain new knowledge through foster parenting conferences and training.
- Turn to professionals such as your child's therapist for advice and consultation.
- Join a network online for foster parents and learn techniques that worked for them.

## Attachment

Areas to examine include:

- sense of emotional closeness to the child
- experience of warmth and affection from the child
- can understand and recognize the child's feelings accurately
- high parental monitoring
- high vigilance towards the child's behaviors and verbalizations
- the child comes to you to express feelings and needs
- the child remains close when strangers are present.

How to increase attachment:

- Improve bonding by meeting the basic and psychological needs (above) of the foster child.
- Write down the positive aspects of your relationship with the child.
- Get more involved in the child's education.
- Increase family time with the child.

## Health

It is important that:

- You as the foster parent are healthy.
- The foster child does not impact negatively on your health.
- Stress does not have a negative effect on your health.

How to reduce health risks:

- Recognize triggers for stress.
- Accept that foster parenting can be stressful.
- Develop healthy stress coping mechanisms (see below).
- Talk to others.
- Discuss with spouse/family members ways of reducing parental stress.
- Use respite care.

### Role control

A lack of role control leads to feelings of helplessness with regard to feeling controlled and dominated by the foster child's needs and demands. To be empowered, you as the foster parent will need to:

- understand where the child is coming from
- recognize that the child is frightened and acting as a caged person
- recognize that the child is fearful of rejection, physical pain, or harsh punishment
- remember that it is not about you, but about the confused and angry child
- be patient despite the odds
- show affection and unconditional acceptance
- recognize that behaviors usually get worse before they get better
- stay calm in the face of anger
- remember to model control over emotions and behavior.

### Empowering the foster parent/foster child relationship

Ask yourself these questions. Discuss them with the other parent, adult children, and the agency:

- How did the child's previous environment affect this child's behaviors and attitudes?
- How is the child handling school, home, friendships, peer relationships, pressures of childhood, and the parent/child relationships?
- What are the child's current stressors?
- How can I help the child cope better?

## 3. Teaching yourself effective parenting styles

There are four primary parenting styles. These are:

- authoritative
- indulgent
- authoritarian (dominating)
- neglectful.

Here we consider only the authoritative parenting style.

### The authoritative parenting style

The authoritative parenting style has four key features:[1]

1. acceptance and warmth
2. willingness to reason
3. an easygoing and responsive interaction style
4. a democratic style of parent/child relationship.

Its characteristics are:

- It is the most nurturing style of parenting.
- It increases social adjustment, competency, self-assurance, and confidence.
- It increases independence in children.
- It increases autonomy in children.
- It develops trust.
- It develops a work ethic.

Research has shown favorable and unfavorable ways of implementing this parenting style.[2]

*Favorable ways of developing an authoritative parenting style*
- Tell the child she/he is important to you.
- Let the child know she/he can talk to you about any problems.
- Teach the child respect by showing them respect.
- Tell the child you appreciate what she/he is trying to accomplish.
- Compliment the child for appropriate behaviors.
- Encourage the child to express her/his opinion.
- Discuss the family rules and the reasons for each rule.
- State your expectations, clarify expectations, and let the child express disagreements.
- If the child misbehaves, give her/him an opportunity to explain why.
- Engage actively with the child while you learn and enjoy her/his company.
- Provide direction for behavior, and remain open to disagreement.
- Listen to the child's desires and wants during family discussions, but make decisions based on family needs and values.

*Unfavorable ways of using the authoritative parenting style*
- Expecting your child to do something immediately without asking questions.
- Always encouraging questioning any time the child does not want to follow family rules.
- Not giving guidelines for acceptable versus unacceptable behaviors.

- Not setting limits because the child is usually well behaved.

- Having the attitude that foster children can do whatever they want freely even if it is not really acceptable to you.

- Wanting to be friends with your foster child, therefore not setting any limits.

### Further training goals

Since the authoritative parenting style has been found to be the most efficacious parenting style, foster parents would benefit from authoritative parenting skills training.

## 4. Enroll in one of the programs available to foster parents

One-third of foster parents in the US give up foster parenting due to disruptive behavior problems in their foster children. A Danish study showed similar results, in which 36 percent of foster parents decided to no longer foster.[3] To prevent losing foster parents, a number of parenting training programs have been developed and are available in some countries. The most popular ones are the Multifamily Treatment Foster Care Program and Team Parenting Program.

The programs rated as the most effective include:

- *Parenting the Strong-Willed Child (PSWC)*. The curriculum of PSWC is a six-week parent education program administered in a group format. It is designed for parents with noncompliant children between the ages of 2–8 years. The program is based on the book *Parenting the Strong Willed Child* and was written with parents in mind. The PSWC program is based on the procedures laid out in "Helping the Noncompliant Child" (below). Parents are taught how to recognize and retrain behaviors that are disruptive. Techniques taught are positive attention for prosocial behaviors; ignoring minor inappropriate behaviors; giving very easy to follow, clear, and concrete instructions to the child; and using appropriate consequences for child behaviors of compliance and noncompliance.

- *Helping the Noncompliant Child.*[4] This is a PMT program that was given the highest evaluation recommendation by the Office of Juvenile Justice and Delinquency Prevention. It was also rated very positively by the Center for Substance Abuse Prevention.

- *The Incredible Years or IY Program.*[5] This program is used with children who are considered to be at risk of conduct problems, juvenile delinquency, and substance abuse. It is a group-administered parent training program. The parent education component to this program involves eight or nine weekly sessions of two hours per session. It has been found to significantly increase positive parent/child interactions and parent/child relationships. The Incredible Years Program is an evidence-based parenting program for parents of young children between three and ten years of age. It was developed to address positive and effective parenting

- *Parent Resources for Information, Development, and Education (PRIDE, CWLA).* This is used in 30 states in the USA and in 19 countries and has been found to increase foster parents' knowledge.

- In Europe, and Africa, it reduced negative disciplining techniques such as spanking and negative statements.

- *Triple P—Positive Parenting Program (PPP).* This program was developed to help foster parents learn specific skills, gain knowledge in preventing serious childhood behavioral and emotional problems, and get trained in five levels of developmental periods in childhood and adolescence. It can be done individually, in a group, or in a self-directed training format. It has been found to reduce foster parent stress and increase confidence and skills.

• *Parent/Child Interaction Therapy (PCIT)*. For foster parents of very young emotionally and behaviorally disordered children between three and six years, this program strengthens the foster parent/child bond, modifies disciplining techniques, improves the child's interpersonal skills, and reduces negative acting-out behaviors. There are 7–10 Relationship Enhancement Phase sessions and 7–10 Behavior Management Phase sessions.

• *Model Approach to Partnerships in Parenting–Group Preparation and Selection of Foster and/or Adoptive Families (MAPP)* is a widely used parenting program.

• *Collaborative Co-Parenting between Biological Parent and Foster Parent.* Given that the goal of removing children is to train the biological parents to change their lifestyles and improve their parenting skills, it makes sense to train the biological parent with the help of the foster parent in a clinical setting. It would be less expensive, more helpful to the child in the long run, and help smooth the transition back into the biological home. It reduces the adversarial good parent–bad parent relationship and puts them on equal footing to collaborate and achieve the same goals of reducing acting-out behaviors in high risk children and improving parent/child relationships. This is a 12-week parenting program.

Additional parenting programs for foster parents that are emerging from evidence-based best practices and their developers are:

• *Nurturing Parenting Program (NPP)*. Increases parenting skills and positive attitudes.

- *Foster Parent Skills Training Program (FPSTP).* Increases sensitivity to the child's needs, acceptance, parent/child bond, and effective parenting skills.

- *Parenting Wisely (PAW).* Computer-based self-administered program reduces conflict.

- *Teaching Family Model (TFM).* Increases family preservation and support, a family-sensitive approach to foster care.

- *Cognitive Behavior Therapy.* Increased emotional and social competence in dealing with difficult behaviors.

- *NOVA, Nova University.* Increased placement stability and licensing rates.[6]

Evidence-based successful therapeutic foster parents' training programs include:

- *Keeping Foster and Kin Parents Supported and Trained (KEEP).* Increased permanency placement,[7] therapeutic foster home placement gains, and good for TFC (treatment foster care) foster parents.

- *NTU Psychotherapy.* Africentric approach for 0–21 years of age. Cultural support and training that improves educational outcomes, mental health, and parent satisfaction.

- *1-2-3 Magic.* Improves compliance and reduces oppositional behaviors in children.

- *Attachment and Biobehavioral Catch-Up (ABC).* Reduces insecure and avoidant attachments.

- *Caring for Infants with Substance Abuse.* Improves knowledge and skills needed.

- *Communication and Conflict Resolution Training.* Improves conflict resolution skills, especially with teens.

- *Family Resilience Project.* Individualized to each foster family and increases positive parenting skills and behaviors.

- *Multidimensional Treatment Foster Care for Preschoolers (MTFC-P).* Meant for 3–6-year-old preschoolers.
- *Multidimensional Treatment Foster Care (MTFC).* This program has been used extensively in Europe as well.

## Notes

1. Chen *et al.* 2011.
2. King *et al.* 2007.
3. Kjeldsen 2010
4. McMahon and Forehand 2005.
5. Webster-Stratton 1991.
6. Licensing rates refers to the financial support given to foster parents who are licensed. In the US, foster parents go through classes to receive licensure to become foster parents,
7. Increased permanancy placement refers to placement in a permanent foster home, in contrast to being moved from one temporary foster home to another.

CHAPTER 8

# THE LETTING GO/ ADOPTING STAGE

## Transitioning Into Own Home/Independent Living

*"You are never too old to set another goal or to dream a new dream."*

—C.S. Lewis

The hardest thing is to let go. This is particularly true for the foster parent who has worked hard to bond with the foster child and watched them challenged but changed. Transitions rarely go smoothly: you go to court, the child goes home or to another placement. Intense anxieties build up in children who come from abused and neglected homes due to their memories of what life used to be like. They begin acting out, being defiant, and difficult to manage. Sometimes, they will start wetting their beds or having nightmares, and their grades in school can also start to drop as their court date nears.

## Pre-adoptive home/long-term placement

If there is a strong family history of mental illness, or parental incapacity due to level of mental retardation, your home can be designated as a pre-adoptive home, or the older teen may be transitioning into an independent living program. In that case, there is no concern regarding transition back into a biological home; the transition will be to independent living and adulthood. However, as a foster parent who is preparing to send the child back to their parents, you can talk to your foster child about going back home and discuss the positive effects while preparing the child to cope with the possible negative effects.

## Effects of transitioning back to the biological home

Factors that affect transitioning back into the biological home include both negative and positive effects.

### Negative effects

These include:

- level of poverty in the biological home
- change of residence to get the children back
- increased exposure to violence
- gang-related involvement
- exposure to drug culture on the streets
- mother's health
- birth of a new sibling
- lack of social support for the family
- loss of therapist and the comforts of foster home
- loss of routines that child is accustomed to
- difference in parenting style that may include spanking with belt and/or verbal abuse
- limited supervision by adults, greater control by older siblings.

## Positive effects

These include:

- no more fear of placement changes
- connection with family ties
- strengthening of attachment bond as mother has done what she needed to get them back
- increased resilience due to foster care placement
- reduced feelings of social isolation and loneliness
- connecting with uncles, aunts, and extended family
- connecting with family cultural values, beliefs, and practices
- living with most if not all the siblings that the child was separated from
- can go for sleepovers to friends and family, can travel
- increased sense of personal control and freedom.

# Transitioning into independent living skills programs

At the age of 16 or 17 years, most states in the USA and other countries plan on transitioning your foster teen to an independent living skills training program. Such programs include:

- safety skills
- social skills
- daily living skills
- sex education
- time management
- work readiness: job skills, time management, promptness, punctuality, computer skills training, interview skills, résumé training, application process, job search and placement

- money management skills: budgeting, having a bank account, and balancing a checkbook
- personal health management skills: personal hygiene, health care needs, and maintaining appointments
- community adjustment skills: budgeting, shopping, and social activities
- transportation: knowing bus/train routes and walking routes
- home management skills: cooking, meal preparation and planning, and home economics.

An interesting study done by the Casey Family Programs National Center for Resource Family Support[1] showed that only 12–18 months after leaving the foster care system:

- of every ten homeless people, three were adults who had been in foster care as children
- almost two-thirds of males and one-tenth of female adults were incarcerated barely three months after being "released" from the foster care system
- one-third were on some form of public assistance and had not finished school
- half were unemployed.

## Maintaining a collaborative relationship with an independent teen/young adult

The statistics above are alarming and very worrying, but not surprising given the information in this and other books. Throughout the independent living program, your teenager would have had the protection of the staff and counselors, holding their hand for most of the time. Once the child graduates, the loss of the state's protective umbrella is sudden and feels great at first, but frightening as time passes.

These foster children who are now almost adults are finally on their own and have no clue how to handle their new-found freedom. Staying in touch with them throughout their transition period despite their refusal to pick up the phone or to call you will help prevent them from falling into the world of homelessness, drug trafficking, teen prostitution, and loneliness. They may call on you for help once again.

## Ways you can help with the transition

Give the child a picture book of all the places you have been to with them, activities they have done, and awards they have won. Include pictures of family, friends, school friends, teachers, and familiar places they have been to. Also, give them examples of their writings, drawings, and work they did at school or home. A special object that they enjoyed at home such as a frame, toy, statue, mug, or other object can be given as part of a 'good luck' parting gift to let them know how special they are and that they can take a part of your home and love with them wherever they might be.

A going-away party with close friends and family is also helpful, with everyone letting them know how special they have been in their lives, and how much they would love to stay in touch. This gives the teen/child permission to call or come by in the future.

Important phone numbers and addresses can also be a part of this going-away packet. Transitioning older teens tend to lose phones and can have them stolen. They will need something more physical like an address book.

Connecting your transitioning teen with your adult children as family will strengthen their relationship and they will have a place they can call home.

It is very important for sibling groups to remain connected through the growing-up years. All efforts should be made to keep them together and families need to be identified that can take in sibling groups and work with them as a unit. They will require specialized training, support, and counseling to keep the unit whole.

A successful foster family can be engaged to mentor a new foster family and assist them in the process of caring for their children. These sessions can be done in group activities in the agency, and the mentor foster families can be recognized with a plaque or special trip sponsored by a local business organization.

## Notes

1. Pecora *et al.* 2005.

# RESOURCES AND USEFUL ADDRESSES

## International

**International Foster Care Organization**
*http://ifco.info*

**International Federation of Educative Communities**
*www.fice-inter.net*

**Child Rights International Network (CRIN)**
*www.crin.org*

**SOS Children's Villages**
*www.sos-childrensvillages.org*


## USA

**Child Welfare Information Gateway**
A comprehensive list of all major foster care support organizations
*www.childwelfare.gov/pubs/reslist/rl_dsp.cfm?subjID=29&rate_chno=11-11267*

**National Foster Parent Association**
*www.nfpainc.org*

**Foster Family Based Treatment Association**
*www.ffta.org*

**Annie E. Casey Foundation**
*www.casey.org*

**Dave Thomas Foundation**
*www.davethomasfoundation.org*

**United States Administration for Children and Families**
*www.acf.hhs.gov/programs/acyf*

**Child Welfare Gateway of America**
*www.childwelfare.gov*

**Child Welfare League of America**
*www.cwla.org*

**Foster Focus Magazine**
*www.Fosterfocusmag.com*

**Fostering Families Today**
*www.fosteringfamiliestoday.com*

**Generations United**
*www.gu.org*

## Canada

**British Columbia Federation of Foster Parent Associations**
*www.fosterparents.com/states3/can.html*

**Canadian Foster Family Association**
*www.canadianfosterfamilyassociation.ca*

Links to state and provincial foster care associations:
*www.canadianfosterfamilyassociation.ca/category/links/#NTL_ASSN*

# UK

**Gov.uk**

UK Government website providing information on government services and information.

*www.gov.uk/foster-carers*

**British Association for Adoption and Fostering**

*www.baaf.org.uk*

**The Fostering Network**

*www.fostering.net*

**Fostering Information Line**

*www.fostering.org.uk*

**Foster Talk**

*www.fostertalk.org*

## Australasia

**The Australian Foster Care Association**

*www.fostercare.org.au/info.html*

**New Zealand Family and Foster Care Federation**

*www.hrs.org.nz/fostercare/FamilyAndFosterCare.htm*

# BIBLIOGRAPHY

AARP (2006) *State Fact Sheets for Grandparents and Other Relatives Raising Children.* Available at www.aarp.org/relationships/grandparenting/info-2006/are search-import-488.html, accessed on 31 December 2012.

AARP (2013) *Grand Facts: State Fact Sheets for Grandparents and Other Relatives Raising Children.* Available at www.aarp.org/relationships/friends-family/grandfacts-sheets, accessed on 26 February 2013.

Administration on Children, Youth and Families—ACYF (2012a) *Promoting Social and Emotional Well-Being for Children and Youth Receiving Child Welfare Services.* Washington, DC: ACYF.

Administration on Children, Youth and Families—ACYF (2012b) "'Too many, too much, too young': red flags on medications and troubled children." *Reclaiming Children and Youth 21,* 2, 59.

AFPA (2006) *Supporting Carers of Other People's Children: A Handbook on Support for Foster, Relative and Kinship Carers and the Children and Young People in Their Care.* Commonwealth of Australia.

APA (2005) *Diagnostic and Statistical Manual of Mental Disorders (DSM-IV).* Arlington, VA: American Psychiatric Association.

Agyemang, A. (2006) *The Michigan Kinship Data Booklet.* Michigan School of Social Work, Michigan State University: Kinship Care Resource Center.

Ahmad, A., Qahar, J., Siddiq, A., Majeed, A., *et al.* (2005) "A 2-year follow-up of orphans' competence, socioemotional problems and post-traumatic stress symptoms in traditional foster care and orphanages in Iraqi Kurdistan." *Child Care Health and Development 31,* 2, 203–215.

Ajduković, M., and Sladović Franz, B. (2005) "Behavioural and emotional problems of children by type of out-of-home care in Croatia." *International Journal of Social Welfare 14,* 3, 163–175.

Albers, E.M., Riksen-Walraven, J.M., and De Weerth, C. (2010) "Developmental stimulation in child care centers contributes to young infants' cognitive development." *Infant Behavior Development 33,* 4, 401–408.

American Academy of Child and Adolescent Psychiatry (2009) *Facts for Families.* Available at http://www.aacap.org/cs/root/facts_for_families/children_with_odd, accessed on 26 February 2013.

Andersson, G. (2012) "Foster care in Sweden: Policy, practice and research." Presentation. Available at www.uni-siegen.de/foster-care-research/network_conferences/3rd_conference/files/gunvor_andersson.pdf, accessed on 21 December 2012.

Annie E. Casey Foundation (2005) *Kinship Care: Supporting Those Who Raise Our Children: Elders as Resources. Intergenerational Strategies Series.* Baltimore, MD: The Annie E. Casey Foundation.

Annie E. Casey Foundation (2012) *Stepping Up for Kids: What Government and Communities Should Do to Support Kinship Families.* KidsCount Data Book 2012. Available at www.aecf.org/~/media/Pubs/Initiatives/KIDS%20COUNT/S/SteppingUpforKids2012PolicyReport/SteppingUpForKidsPolicyReport2012.pdf, accessed on 27 April 2013.

Anon. (1998) "Early child care and self-control, compliance, and problem behavior at twenty-four and thirty-six months." *Child Development 69,* 4, 1145–1170.

Anon. (2003) "Does amount of time spent in child care predict socioemotional adjustment during the transition to kindergarten?" *Child Development 74,* 4, 976–1005.

Anon. (2004) "Are child developmental outcomes related to before- and after-school care arrangements? Results from the NICHD Study of Early Child Care." *Child Development 75,* 1, 280–295.

Armsden, G., Pecora, P., Payne, V., and Szatkiewicz, J. (2000) "Children placed in long term foster care: an intake profile using the child behavior checklist/4-18." *Journal of Emotional and Behavioral Disorders 8,* 1, 49–65.

Barlow, J., Parsons, J., and Stewart-Brown, S. (2005) "Preventing emotional and behavioural problems." *Child Care 31,* 1, 33–42.

Barth, R.P., Crea, T.M., John, K., Thoburn, J., and Quinton, D. (2005) "Beyond attachment theory and therapy: towards sensitive and evidence-based practice principles and practices for services to foster and adoptive families." *Child and Family Social Work 10,* 257–268.

Barth, R.P., Lloyd, E.C., Green, R.L., James, S., Leslie, L.K., and Landsverk, J. (2007) "Predictors of placement moves among children with and without emotional and behavioral disorders." *Journal of Emotional and Behavioral Disorders 15,* 46.

Barth, R.P., Wildfire, J., and Green, R.L. (2006) "Placement into foster care and the interplay of urbanicity, child behavior problems, and poverty." *The American Journal of Orthopsychiatry 76,* 3, 358–366.

Barth, R.P., Yeaton, J., and Winterfelt, N. (1994) "Psychoeducational Groups with Foster Parents of Sexually Abused Children." *Child Adolescent Social Work Journal 11,* 5, 405–424.

Bass, S., Shields, M.K., and Behrman, R.E. (2004) "Children, families, and foster care: analysis and recommendations." *Children, Families, and Foster Care 14,* 1, 4–29.

Begun, A.L. (1995) "Sibling relationships and foster care placements for young children." *Early Child Development and Care 106,* 1, 237–250.

Belcher, J.R. (1987) "Adult foster care: an alternative to homelessness for some chronically mentally ill persons." *Adult Foster Care Journal 1,* 4, 212–225.

Bernier, A., and Dozier, M. (2003) "Bridging the attachment transmission gap: the role of maternal mind-mindedness." *International Journal of Behavioral Development 27,* 4, 355–365.

Berrick, J.D., Courtney, A., and Barth, R.P. (1993) "Specialized foster care and group home care: similarities and differences in the characteristics of children in care." *Children and Youth Services Review 15*, 6, 453–473.

Beutler, L.E., Williams, R.E., and Zetzer, H.A. (2009) "Efficacy of treatment for victims of child sexual abuse." *The Future of Children Center for the Future of Children the David and Lucile Packard Foundation 4*, 2, 156–175.

Bowlby, J. (1969) *Attachment and Loss. Vol. 1: Attachment.* New York: Basic Books.

Broady, T.R., Stoyles, G.J., McMullan, K., Caputi, P., and Crittenden, N. (2009) "The experiment of foster care." *Journal of Child and Family Studies 19*, 5, 559–571.

Bryderup, I.M. (2008) *Summary for Denmark—Project Yippee.* Available at http://tcru.ioe.ac.uk/yippee/Portals/1/Denmark%20summary.pdf, accessed on 21 December 2012.

Buehler, C., Rhodes, K.W., Orme, J.G., and Cuddeback, G. (2006) "The potential for successful family foster care: conceptualizing competency domains for foster parents." *Child Welfare 85*, 3, 523–558.

Buffington, K., Dierkhising, C.B., and Marsh, S.C. (2010) *Ten Things Every Juvenile Court Judge Should Know About Trauma and Delinquency.* Technical Assistance Bulletin, National Council of Juvenile and Family Court Judges, 1–18.

Bunge, M. (1981) "Development indicators." *World Development 9*, 3, 249–271.

Byrne, C., Browne, G., Roberts, J., Gafhi, A., *et al.* (2004) "Adolescent emotional/behavioral problems and risk behavior in Ontario primary care: comorbidities and costs." *Health San Francisco 8*, 3, 135–144.

Cabrera, P., Auslander, W., and Polgar, M. (2009) "Future orientation of adolescents in foster care: relationship to trauma, mental health, and HIV risk behaviors." *Journal of Child Adolescent Trauma 2*, 4, 271–286.

Caltabiano, M.L., and Thorpe, R. (2007) "Attachment style of foster carers and caregiving role performance." *Child Care in Practice 13*, 2, 137–148.

Cameron, P. (2005) "Child molestations by homosexual foster parents: Illinois, 1997–2002." *Psychological Reports 96*, 1, 227–230.

Canali, C., and Vecchiato, T. (2009) "Foster care in Italy: Policy, structure and research." *Third International Network Conference Foster Care Research*, 21–23. Rorschach: Fondazione Emanuela Zancan, Padova, Italy.

Cappelletty, G.G., Mackie Brown, M., and Shumate, S.E. (2005) "Correlates of the Randolph Attachment Disorder Questionnaire (RADQ) in a sample of children in foster placement." *Child and Adolescent Social Work Journal 22*, 1, 71–84.

Centers for Disease Control and Prevention (2012) "Alcohol use and binge drinking among women of childbearing age—United States, 2006–2010." *Weekly MMR 61*, 28, 534–528.

Chamberlain, P. (2003a) "Antisocial Behavior and Delinquency in Girls." In P. Chamberlain (ed.) *Treating Chronic Juvenile Offenders: Advances Made Through the Oregon Multidimensional Treatment Foster Care Model.* Washington, DC: American Psychological Association.

Chamberlain, P. (2003b) "An Application of Multidimensional Treatment Foster Care for Early Intervention." In P. Chamberlain (ed.) *Treating Chronic Juvenile Offenders: Advances Made Through the Oregon Multidimensional Treatment Foster Care Model.* Washington, DC: American Psychological Association.

Chamberlain, P. (2003c) "An Overview of the History and Development of the Multidimensional Treatment Foster Care Model and the Supporting Research." In P. Chamberlain (ed.) *Treating Chronic Juvenile Offenders: Advances Made Through the Oregon Multidimensional Treatment Foster Care Model.* Washington, DC: American Psychological Association.

Chamberlain, P. (2003d) "The Development of Antisocial Behavior." In P. Chamberlain (ed.) *Treating Chronic Juvenile Offenders: Advances Made Through the Oregon Multidimensional Treatment Foster Care Model.* Washington, DC: American Psychological Association.

Chamberlain, P., Leve, L.D., and Smith, D.K. (2006) "Preventing behavior problems and health-risking behaviors in girls in foster care." *International Journal of Behavioral Consultation and Therapy 2*, 4, 518–530.

Chamberlain, P., Price, J., Leve, L.D., Laurent, H., Landsverk, J.A., and Reid, J.B. (2008) "Prevention of behavior problems for children in foster care: outcomes and mediation effects." *Prevention Science 9*, 1, 17–27.

Chambers, M.F., Saunders, A.M., New, B.D., Williams, C.L., and Stachurska, A. (2010) "Assessment of children coming into care: processes, pitfalls and partnerships." *Clinical Child Psychology and Psychiatry 15*, 4, 511–527.

Chen, S.H., Zhou, Q., Eisenberg, N., Valiente, C., and Wang, Y. (2011) "Parental expressivity and parenting styles in Chinese families: prospective and unique relations to children's psychological adjustment." *Parenting 11*, 4, 288–307.

Chen, X., Hastings, P.D., Rubin, K.H., Chen, H., Cen, G., and Stewart, S.L. (1998) "Child-rearing attitudes and behavioral inhibition in Chinese and Canadian toddlers: a cross-cultural study." *Developmental Psychology 34*, 4, 677–686.

Child Welfare Information Gateway (2010a) *Definitions of Child Abuse and Neglect in Federal Law.* Washington, DC: US Department of Health and Human Services, Administration for Children and Families. Available at www.childwelfare. gov/can/defining/federal.cfm, accessed on 28 January 2013.

Child Welfare Information Gateway (2010b) *Placement of Children With Relatives.* Washington, DC: US Department of Health and Human Services, Administration for Children, Youth and Families, Children's Bureau.

Child Welfare Information Gateway (2012) *Foster Care Statistics 2010. Child Welfare Information Gateway.* Washington, DC: US Department of Health and Human Services, Administration for Children, Youth and Families, Children's Bureau.

Chipungu, S.S., and Bent-Goodley, T.B. (2004) "Meeting the challenges of contemporary foster care." *The Future of Children/Center for the Future of Children the David and Lucile Packard Foundation 14*, 1, 74–93.

Choudhury, S., Charman, A., and Blakemore, S.J. (2008) "Development of the teenage brain." *Mind Brain and Education 2*, 3, 142–147.

Clausen, J.M., Landsverk, J., Ganger, W., Chadwick, D., and Litrownik, A. (1998) "Mental health problems of children in foster care." *Journal of Child and Family Studies 7*, 3, 283–296.

Cloitre, M., Stolbach, B.C., Herman, J.L., Pynoos, R., Wang, J., and Petkova, E. (2009) "A developmental approach to complex PTSD: childhood and adult cumulative trauma as predictors of symptom complexity." *Journal of Traumatic Stress 22*, 5, 399–408.

Committee on Early Childhood, Adoption and Dependent Care (2000) "Developmental issues for young children in foster care." *Pediatrics 106*, 5, 1145–1150.

Conduct Problems Prevention Research Group (2002) "Evaluation of the first 3 years of the Fast Track prevention trial with children at high risk for adolescent conduct problems." *Journal of Abnormal Child Psychology 30*, 1, 19–35.

Conduct Problems Prevention Research Group (2010) "The effects of a multiyear universal social-emotional learning program: the role of student and school characteristics." *Journal of Consulting and Clinical Psychology 78*, 156–168.

Conduct Problems Prevention Research Group (2011) "The effects of the Fast Track preventive intervention on the development of conduct disorder across childhood." *Child Development 82*, 331–345.

Connecticut Department of Children and Families (2011) *We All Need Somebody: Supporting Children, Families and the Workforce in Connecticut's Family Foster Care System*. A Report in the "Fostering the Future" Series. Available at www. ct.gov/dcf/lib/dcf/publications/pdf/final_family_foster_report_9_30_11. pdf, accessed on 22 December 2012.

Cook, A., *et al.* (2007) "Complex trauma in children and adolescents." *Focal Point, Research, Policy, and Practice in Children's Mental Health 21*, 1, 4–8.

Courtney, M., Dworsky, A., Lee, J., and Raap, M. (2010) *Midwest Evaluation of the Adult Functioning of Former Foster Youth : Outcomes at Ages 23 and 24*. Chicago: Chapin Hall at the University of Chicago.

Cox, M.E., Cherry, D.J., and Orme, J.G. (2011) "Measuring the willingness to foster children with emotional and behavioral problems." *Children and Youth Services Review 33*, 1, 59–65.

Crum, W. (2010) "Foster parent parenting characteristics that lead to increased placement stability or disruption." *Children and Youth Services Review 32*, 2, 185–190.

CWLA (n.d.) *The PRIDE Model of Practice*. Available at www.cwla.org/programs/ trieschman/pride.htm, accessed on 31 December 2012.

D'Andrea, W., Ford, J., Stolbach, B., Spinazzola, J., and van der Kolk, B.A. (2012) "Understanding interpersonal trauma in children: why we need a developmentally appropriate trauma diagnosis." *The American Journal of Orthopsychiatry 82*, 2, 187–200.

Daigneault, I., Cyr, M., and Tourigny, M. (2003) "Psychological profile of adolescent girl victims of sexual abuse and under the protection of Child Services." *Sante Mentale Au Quebec 28*, 2, 211–232.

Darlington, Y., and Feeney, J.A. (2008) "Collaboration between mental health and child protection services: professionals' perceptions of best practice." *Children and Youth Services Review 30*, 2, 187–198.

Daro, D.A. (1994) "Prevention of child sexual abuse." *The Future of Children/Center for the Future of Children the David and Lucile Packard Foundation 4*, 2, 198–223.

de Arellano, M.A., Ko, S.J., Danielson, C.K., and Sprague, C.M. (2008) *Trauma-informed Interventions: Clinical and Research Evidence and Culture-specific Information Project.* Los Angeles, CA and Durham, NC: National Center for Child Traumatic Stress. Available at nctsn.org/nctsn_assets/pdfs/CCG_Book.pdf, accessed 27 February 2013.

Demick, J., and Andreoletti, C. (2003) "'Roots that Clutch': What Adoption and Foster Care Can Tell Us about Adult Development." In J. Demick and C. Andreoletti (eds) *The Handbook of Adult Development.* New York: Kluwer Academic/Plenum Publishers.

Denmark's Third Report (2004) *Children in Public Out-Of-Home Care in Denmark.* Available at www.uea.ac.uk/polopoly_fs/1.85253!denmark%20report.pdf, accessed on 22 December 2012.

Denuwelaere, M., and Bracke, P. (2007) "Support and conflict in the foster family and children's well-being: a comparison between foster and birth children." *Family Relations 56*, 1, 67–79.

Dietrich, A.M., Smiley, W.C., and Frederick, C. (2007) "The roles of childhood maltreatment and psychopathy in sexual recidivism of treated sex offenders." *Journal of Aggression Maltreatment Trauma 14*, 3, 19–31.

Doelling, J.L., and Johnson, J.H. (1990) "Predicting success in foster placement: the contribution of parent-child temperament characteristics." *The American Journal of Orthopsychiatry 60*, 4, 585–593.

Dozier, M., Lindhiem, O., Lewis, E., Bick, J., Bernard, K., and Peloso, E. (2009) "Effects of a foster parent training program on young children's attachment behaviors: preliminary evidence from a randomized clinical trial." *Child and Adolescent Social Work Journal 26*, 4, 321–332.

Dozier, M., Stovall, K.C., Albus, K.E., and Bates, B. (2001) "Attachment for infants in foster care: the role of caregiver state of mind." *Child Development 72*, 5, 1467–1477.

Eggertsen, L. (2008) *Primary Factors Related to Multiple Placements for Children in Out-of-Home Care.* Washington, DC: Child Welfare League of America.

Ellingsen, I.T., Shemmings, D., and Størksen, I. (2011) "The concept of 'family' among Norwegian adolescents in long-term foster care." *Child and Adolescent Social Work Journal 28*, 4, 301–318.

Ellonen, N., and Pösö, T. (2011) "Violence experiences in care: some methodological remarks based on the Finnish child victim survey." *Child Abuse Review 20*, 3, 197–212.

Farmer, E.M.Z., Burns, B.J., Dubs, M.S., and Thompson, S. (2002) "Assessing conformity to standards for treatment foster care." *Journal of Emotional and Behavioral Disorders 10*, 4, 213–222.

Farmer, E.M.Z., Burns, B.J., Wagner, H.R., Murray, M., and Southerland, D.G. (2010) "Enhancing 'usual practice' treatment foster care: findings from a randomized trial on improving youths' outcomes." *Psychiatric Services 61*, 6, 555–561.

Farmer, E.M.Z., Mustillo, S.A., Wagner, H.R., Burns, B.J., *et al.* (2010) "Service use and multi-sector use for mental health problems by youth in contact with child welfare." *Children and Youth Services Review 32*, 6, 815–821.

Fechter-Leggett, M.O., and O'Brien, K. 2010. "The effects of kinship care on adult mental health outcomes of alumni of foster care." *Children and Youth Services Review 32*, 2, 206–213.

Firdion, J.-M. (2003) *Homelessness, Poverty and Foster Care.* Paper presented at Social Exclusion Inequality and Health Workshop, Brown University, Providence, June 4, 2003. Available at www.brown.edu/Departments/Sociology/faculty/silver/sirs/papers/firdion.pdf, accessed on 24 December 2012.

Fisher, P.A., and Chamberlain, P. (2000) "Multidimensional treatment foster care: a program for intensive parenting, family support, and skill building." *Journal of Emotional and Behavioral Disorders 8*, 3, 155–164.

Fisher, P.A., Chamberlain, P., and Leve, L.D. (2009) "Improving the lives of foster children through evidenced-based interventions." *Vulnerable Children and Youth Studies 4*, 2, 122–127.

Fisher, P.A., Stoolmiller, M., Mannering, A.M., Takahashi, A., and Chamberlain, P. (2011) "Foster placement disruptions associated with problem behavior: mitigating a threshold effect." *Journal of Consulting and Clinical Psychology 79*, 4, 481–487.

Flanagan-Howard, R., Carr, A., Shevlin, M., Dooley, B., *et al.* (2009) "Development and initial validation of the institutional child abuse processes and coping inventory among a sample of Irish adult survivors of institutional abuse." *Child Abuse Neglect 33*, 9, 586–597.

Frey, L., Cushing, G., Freundlich, M., and Brenner, E. (2008) "Achieving permanency for youth in foster care: assessing and strengthening emotional security." *Child and Family Social Work 13*, 2, 218–226.

Furlong, M., McGilloway, S., Bywater, T., Hutchings, J., *et al.* (2010) "Behavioural and cognitive-behavioural group-based parenting programmes for early-onset conduct problems in children aged 3 to 12 years." *Cochrane Database of Systematic Reviews 2012, Issue 2.* Art. No.: CD008225.

Gallico, R.P., Burns, T.J., and Grob, C.S. (1988) *Emotional and Behavioral Problems in Children with Learning Disabilities.* Boston: College-Hill Press/Little, Brown & Co.

Garber, K.B., Visootsak, J., and Warren, S.T. (2008) "Fragile X Syndrome." *European Journal of Human Genetics 16*, 6, 666–672.

Gardner, D. (2008) *Youth Aging Out of Foster Care: Identifying Strategies and Best Practices.* Seattle, WA: Casey Family Programs. Available at www.dshs.wa.gov/pdf/ca/YouthAgingoutofFoster.pdf, accessed on 24 December 2012.

Garland, A.F., Hough, R.L., Landsverk, J.A., Mccabe, K.M., *et al.* (2000) "Racial and ethnic variations in mental health care utilization among children in foster care." *Children's Services: Social Policy, Research, and Practice 3*, 3, 133–146.

Ghera, M.M., Marshall, P.J., Fox, N.A., Zeanah, C.H., *et al.* (2009) "The effects of foster care intervention on socially deprived institutionalized children's attention and positive affect: results from the BEIP study." *Journal of Child Psychology and Psychiatry, and Allied Disciplines 50*, 3, 246–253.

Golden, J.A. (2009) "Introduction to a special issue on the assessment of children with reactive attachment disorder and the treatment of children with attachment difficulties or a history of maltreatment and/or foster care." *Behavioural Development Bulletin 15*, 1–4.

Golding, K. (2007) "Attachment theory as a support for foster carers and adoptive parents." *Adoption and Fostering 31*, 2, 77–79.

Gramkowski, B., Kools, S., Paul, S., Boyer, C.B., Monasterio, E., and Robbins, N. (2009) "Health risk behavior of youth in foster care." *Journal of Child and Adolescent Psychiatric Nursing 22*, 2, 77–85.

Grandits, H., and Heady, P. (eds) (2010) *Family, Kinship and State in Contemporary Europe. Vol. 1: The Century of Welfare: Eight Countries*. Frankfurt: Campus.

Greene, B., and Pilowsky, D. (1994) "The abused and neglected foster child: determinants of emotional conflict and oppositional behavior." *Journal of Social Distress and the Homeless 3*, 3, 283–297.

Greeson, J.K.P., Briggs, E.C., Kisiel, C.L., Layne, C.M., *et al.* (2011) "Complex trauma and mental health in children and adolescents placed in foster care: findings from the National Child Traumatic Stress Network." *Child Welfare 90*, 6, 91–108.

Griffin, G., McEwen, E., Samuels, B.H., Suggs, H., Redd, J.L., and McClelland, G.M. (2011) "Infusing protective factors for children in foster care." *The Psychiatric Clinics of North America 34*, 1, 185–203.

Grimm, W., and Darwall, J. (2005) "Foster parents: who are they? Reality v. perception." *Youth Law News XXVI*, 3, 1–8.

Hadfield, S.C., and Preece, P.M. (2008) "Obesity in looked after children: is foster care protective from the dangers of obesity?" *Child Care Health and Development 34*, 6, 710–712.

Haight, W., Kagle, D., and Black, J.E. (2003) "Understanding and supporting parent–child visits: attachment theory and research." *Social Work 48*, 2, 195–295.

Hammerschlag, M.R. (1998) "The transmissibility of sexually transmitted diseases in sexually abused children." *Child Abuse Neglect 22*, 6, 623–635; discussion 637–643.

Harden, B.J., Meisch, A.d'A., Vick, J.E., and Pandohie-Johnson, L. (2008) "Measuring parenting among foster families: the development of the Foster Parent Attitudes Questionnaire (FPAQ)." *Children and Youth Services Review 30*, 8, 879–892.

Healey, C.V., and Fisher, P.A. (2011) "Young children in foster care and the development of favorable outcomes." *Children and Youth Services Review 33*, 10, 1822–1830.

Herczog, M., Van Pagee, R., and Pasztor, E.M. (2001) "The multinational transfer of competency-based foster parent assessment, selection, and training: a nine-country case study." *Child Welfare 80*, 5, 631–644.

Holtan, A., Rønning, J.A., Handegård, B.H., and Sourander, A. (2005) "A comparison of mental health problems in kinship and nonkinship foster care." *European Child Adolescent Psychiatry 14*, 4, 200–207.

Huntsinger, C.S., and Jose, P.E. (2009) "Relations among parental acceptance and control and children's social adjustment in Chinese American and European American families." *Journal of Family Psychology 23*, 3, 321–330.

Illinois Childhood Trauma Coalition (n.d.) *Core Competencies for Professional Development on Childhood Trauma.* Chicago, Il: Illinois Childhood Trauma Coalition. Available at http://illinoischildhoodtrauma.org/files/ICTC%20 Critical%20Learnings%20for%20Professional%20Development%20 4-12%20(2).pdf, accessed on 24 December 2012.

International Federation of Educative Communities (n.d.) *Quality4Children Standards for Out-of-Home Child Care in Europe.* Available at www.quality4children. info/navigation/cms,id,31,nodeid,31,_language,en.html, accessed on 24 December 2012.

Jaffe, E.D. (1969) "Child welfare in Israel: an overview." *The Hebrew University, Jerusalem, Israel 33*, 170–182. Available at http://bjpa.org/Publications/ downloadPublication.cfm?PublicationID=1657, accessed on 24 December 2012.

Jakušovaitė, I., Darulis, Z., and Žekas, R. (2005) "Lithuanian health care in transitional state: ethical problems." *BMC Public Health 5*, 117.

James, S., Leslie, L.K., Hurlbert, M.S., Slymen, D.J., *et al.* (2006) "Children in out-of-home care: entry into intensive or restrictive mental health and residential care placements." *Journal of Emotional and Behavioral Disorders 14*, 4, 196–208.

Jee, S.H., Conn, A.-M., Szilagyi, P.G., Blumkin, A., Baldwin, C.D., and Szilagyi, M.A. (2010) "Identification of social-emotional problems among young children in foster care." *The Journal of Child Psychology and Psychiatry and Allied Disciplines 51*, 12, 1351–1358.

Johnson, H. (2005) *Literature Review of Foster Care.* Moshi, Kilimanjaro Region, Tanzania: Mkombozi Centre for Street Children. Available at www. mkombozi.org/publications/research_report/2005_08_research_report_ fostering_literature.pdf, accessed on 24 December 2012.

Johnson-Garner, M.Y., and Meyers, S.A. (2003) "What factors contribute to the resilience of African-American children within kinship care?" *Child and Youth Care Forum 32*, 5, 255–269.

Jones, G., and Morrissette, P.J. (1999) "Foster parent stress." *Canadian Journal of Counselling 33*, 1, 13–27.

Jordan, P.J., and Lawrence, S.A. (2009) "Emotional intelligence in teams: development and initial validation of the short version of the Workgroup Emotional Intelligence Profile (WEIP-S)." *Journal of Management 15*, 4, 452–469. Available at http://ejournal.narotama.ac.id/files/jmo.15.4.452.pdf, accessed on 24 December 2012.

Kaehler, L.A., and Freyd, J.J. (2011) "Betrayal trauma and borderline personality characteristics: gender differences." *Psychological Trauma Theory Research Practice and Policy 4*, 4, 379–385.

Kaplan, D.W., Feinstein, R.A., Fisher, M.M., Klein, J.D., *et al.* (2001) "Care of the adolescent sexual assault victim." *Pediatrics 107*, 6, 1476–1479.

Karp, R.J. (2011) "Response to Bell *et al.* ['The remarkably high prevalence of epilepsy and seizure history in fetal alcohol spectrum disorders.' *Alcohol Clin Exp Res 34*, 1084–1089]." *Alcoholism, Clinical and Experimental Research 35*, 6, 1017–1018; author reply 1019.

Kidscount (2011) *America's Children, America's Challenge: Promoting Opportunity for the Next Generation.* Baltimore, MD: The Annie E. Casey Foundation. Available at datacentre.kidscount.org/databook/2011, accessed on 27 April 2013.

King, K.A., Kramer, L., Bernard, A., and Vidourek, R. (2007) "Foster parents' involvement in authoritative parenting and interest in future parenting training." *Journal of Child and Family Studies 16*, 5, 606–614.

Kjeldsen, C. (2010) "When family becomes the job: fostering practice in Denmark." *Adoption and Fostering 34*, 1, 52–64.

Koponen, A.M., Kalland, M., and Autti-Rämö, I. (2009) "Caregiving environment and socio-emotional development of foster-placed FASD-children." *Children and Youth Services Review 31*, 9, 1049–1056.

Kretchmar, M.D., Worsham, N.L., and Swenson, N. (2005) "Anna's story: a qualitative analysis of an at-risk mother's experience in an attachment-based foster care program." *Attachment and Human Development 7*, 1, 31–49.

Krystal, H. (1995) "Disorders of Emotional Development in Addictive Behavior." In S. Dowling (ed.) *The Psychology and Treatment of Addictive Behavior.* Madison, CT: International Universities Press.

Kutz, G.D. (2011) *Foster children: HHS Guidance Could Help States Improve Oversight of Psychotropic Prescriptions.* Washington, DC: Government Accountability Office. Available at www.gao.gov/assets/590/586570.pdf, accessed on 24 December 2012.

Landsverk, J.A., Burns, B.J., Stambaugh, L.F., and Reutz, J.A.R. (2005) "Psychosocial interventions for children and adolescents in foster care: review of research literature." *Child Welfare 88*, 1, 49–69.

Lawrence, C.R., Carlson, E.A., and Egeland, B. (2006) "The impact of foster care on development." *Development and Psychopathology 18*, 1, 57–76.

Layne, C.M., Ippen, C.G., Strand, V., Stuber, M., *et al.* (2011) "The core curriculum on childhood trauma: a tool for training a trauma-informed workforce." *Psychological Trauma Theory Research Practice and Policy 3*, 3, 243–252.

Leathers, S.J. (2003) "Parental visiting, conflicting allegiances, and emotional and behavioral problems among foster children." *Family Relations 52*, 1, 53–63.

Leathers, S.J. (2006) "Placement disruption and negative placement outcomes among adolescents in long-term foster care: the role of behavior problems." *Child Abuse Neglect 30*, 3, 307–324.

Leve, L.D., Fisher, P.A., and Degarmo, D.S. (2007) "Peer relations at school entry: sex differences in the outcomes of foster care." *Merrill-Palmer Quarterly 53*, 4, 557–577.

Leyendecker, B., Lamb, M.E., and Schölmerich, A. (1997) "Studying mother–infant interaction: the effects of context and length of observation in two subcultural groups." *Infant Behavior and Development 20*, 3, 325–337.

Lie, G.Y., and McMurtry, S.L. (1991) "Foster care for sexually abused children: a comparative study." *Child Abuse Neglect 15*, 1–2, 111–121.

Littrell, J., and Lyons, P. (2010) "Pediatric bipolar disorder: an issue for child welfare." *Children and Youth Services Review 32*, 7, 965–973.

Lloyd, E.C., and Barth, R.P. (2011) "Developmental outcomes after five years for foster children returned home, remaining in care, or adopted." *Children and Youth Services Review 33*, 8, 1383–1391.

Longshore, D. (1998) "Self-control and criminal opportunity: a prospective test of the general theory of crime." *Social Problems 45*, 1, 102–113.

Malhotra, S., and Biswas, P. (2006) "Behavioral and psychological assessment of child sexual abuse in clinical practice." *International Journal of Behavioral Consultation and Therapy 2*, 1, 12.

Manente, C.J., Maraventano, J.C., LaRue, R.H., Delmolino, L., and Sloan, D. (2009) "Effective behavioral intervention for adults on the autism spectrum: best practices in functional assessment and treatment development." *Behavior Analyst 11*, 1, 36–49.

Mäntymaa, M., Puura, K., Luoma, I., Salmelin, R.K., and Tamminen, T. (2004) "Early mother–infant interaction, parental mental health and symptoms of behavioral and emotional problems in toddlers." *Infant Behavior and Development 27*, 2, 134–149.

Marinkovic, J., and Backovic, D. (2007) "Relationship between type of placement and competencies and problem behavior of adolescents in long-term foster care." *Children and Youth Services Review 29*, 2, 216–225.

Martin, E.D., Altemeier, W.A., Hickson, G.B., Davis, A., and Glascoe, F.P. (1992) "Improving resources for foster care." *Clinical Pediatrics 31*, 7, 400–404.

McCoy, D.C., and Raver, C.C. (2011) "Caregiver emotional expressiveness, child emotion regulation, and child behavior problems among Head Start families." *Social Development 20*, 4, 741–761.

Mccrae, J.S. (2009) "Emotional and behavioral problems reported in child welfare over 3 years." *Journal of Emotional and Behavioral Disorders 17*, 1, 17–28.

McMahon, R.J. and Forehand, R.L. (2005) *Helping the Noncompliant Child: Family-Based Treatment for Oppositional Behaviour.* New York, NY: Guildford Press.

McWey, L. (2001) "I promise to act better if you let me see my family: attachment theory and foster care visitation." *Journal of Family Social Work 5*, 1, 91–106.

Medicaid Medical Directors Learning Network and Rutgers Center for Education and Research on Mental Health Therapeutics (2010) *Antipsychotic Medication Use in Medicaid Children and Adolescents: Report and Resource Guide from a 16-State Study.* MMDLN/Rutgers CERTs Publication #1. Available at http://rci.rutgers.edu/~cseap/MMDLNAPKIDS.html, accessed on 26 December 2010.

Milan, S.E., and Pinderhughes, E.E. (2000) "Factors influencing maltreated children's early adjustment in foster care." *Development and Psychopathology 12,* 1, 63–81.

Millward, R., Kennedy, E., Towlson, K., and Minnis, H. (2006) "Reactive attachment disorder in looked-after children." *Emotional and Behavioural Difficulties 11,* 4, 273–279.

Morgan, K., and Baron, R. (2011) "Challenging behaviour in looked after young people, feelings of parental self-efficacy and psychological well-being in foster carers." *Adoption and Fostering 35,* 1, 18–32.

Morrissette, P.J. (1994) "Foster parenting: a developmental model." *Child and Adolescent Social Work Journal 11,* 3, 235–246.

Morrissette, P.J. (1996) "Family therapist as consultant in foster care: expanding the parameters of practice." *The American Journal of Family Therapy 24,* 1, 55–64.

Murray, M.M., Southerland, D., Farmer, E.M., and Ballentine, K. (2010) "Enhancing and adapting treatment foster care: lessons learned in trying to change practice." *Journal of Child and Family Studies 19,* 4 393–403.

National Working Group on Foster Care and Education (2011) *Education is the Lifeline for Youth in Foster Care: Research Highlights on Education and Foster Care.* Baltimore, MD: Annie E. Casey Programs.

Nesmith, A. (2006) "Predictors of running away from family foster care." *Child Welfare 85,* 3, 585–609.

Newcomer, P.L., Barenbaum, E., and Pearson, N. (1995) "Depression and anxiety in children and adolescents with learning disabilities, conduct disorders, and no disabilities." *Journal of Emotional and Behavioral Disorders 3,* 1, 27–39.

NICHD Early Child Care Research Network (1997) "The effects of infant child care on infant–mother attachment security: results of the NICHD study of early child care." *Child Development 68,* 5, 860–879.

NICHD Early Child Care Research Network (2003) "Early child care and mother–child interaction from 36 months through first grade." *Infant Behavior and Development 26,* 3, 345–370.

Nordmark, E., Josenby, A.L., Lagergren, J. Andersson, G., Strömblad, L.-G., and Westbom, L. (2008) "Long-term outcomes five years after selective dorsal rhizotomy." *BMC Pediatrics 8,* 54.

Northern California Training Academy (2008) *A Literature Review of Placement Stability in Child Welfare Service: Issues, Concerns, Outcomes and Future Directions.* Davis, CA: UC Davis, The Center for Human Services. Available at www.childsworld.ca.gov/res/pdf/PlacementStability.pdf, accessed on 22 December 2012.

NSPCC (2011) *Child Abuse and Neglect in the UK Today.* Available at www.nspcc. org.uk/Inform/research/findings/child_abuse_neglect_wda84173.html, accessed on 26 February 2013.

NSPCC (2012) *An Introduction to Child Neglect.* Available at www.nspcc.org.uk/ Inform/resourcesforprofessionals/neglect/introduction_wda90252.html, accessed on 27 December 2012.

Oliván Gonzalvo, G. (2003) "Children and adolescents in foster care: health problems and guidelines for their health care." *Anales De Pediatria 58,* 2, 128–135.

Olusanya, B., and Hodes, D. (2000) "West African children in private foster care in City and Hackney." *Child Care Health and Development 26,* 4, 337–342.

Orme, J.G., Cuddeback, G.S., Buehler, C., Cox, M.E., and Le Prohn, N.S. (2006) "Measuring foster parent potential: Casey Foster Parent Inventory-Applicant Version." *Research on Social Work Practice 17,* 1, 77–92.

Pacifici, C., Delaney, R., White, L., Nelson, C., and Cummings, K. (2006) "Web-based training for foster, adoptive, and kinship parents." *Children and Youth Services Review 28,* 11, 1329–1343.

Payne, H. (2009) "Disabled Children Living Away from Home in the Care System: Coordinating Medical and Health Services." In C. Burns (ed.) *Disabled Children Living Away from Home in Foster Care and Residential Settings.* London: Mac Keith Press.

Peake, L., and Townsend, L. (2012) *The Motivations to Foster: A Toolkit for Fostering Services.* London: The Fostering Network.

Pecora, P.J., and O'Brien, K. (2007) *American Indian/Alaska Native Findings from the Casey National Study.* Available at www.casey.org/Resources/Publications/ pdf/AmericanIndianAlaskaNative.pdf, accessed on 24 December 2012.

Pecora, P.J., Jensen, P.S., Romanelli, L.H., Jackson, L.J., and Ortiz, A. (2009) "Mental health services for children placed in foster care: an overview of current challenges." *Child Welfare 88,* 1, 5–26.

Pecora, P.J., Kessler, R.C., Williams, J., O'Brien, K., *et al.* (2005) *Improving Family Foster Care: Findings from the Northwest Foster Care Alumni Study.* Seattle, WA: Casey Family Programs. Available at www.casey.org/Resources/Publications/ ImprovingFamilyFosterCare.htm, accessed on 24 December 2012.

Pederson, D.R. *et al.* (1992) "Maternal sensitivity and attachment security: concordance of home- and lab-based measures." *Child Development 13.*

Perry, B.D., and Hambrick, E.P. (2008) "The neurosequential model of therapeutics." *Reclaiming Children and Youth 17,* 3, 38–43.

Pine, D. (2012) *Transient vs. Persistent Anxiety.* Available at www.dailymotion.com/ video/xpf4yx_transient-vs-persistent-anxiety_lifestyle, accessed on 27 April 2013.

Polgar, M., and Auslander, W. (2009) "HIV prevention for youths in foster care: understanding future orientation and intended risk behaviors." *Journal of HIVAIDS Social Services 8,* 4, 397–413.

Ponciano, L. (2010) "Attachment in foster care: the role of maternal sensitivity, adoption, and foster mother experience." *Child and Adolescent Social Work Journal 27*, 2, 97–114.

Preston, S., Yates, K., and Moss, M. (2012) "Does emotional resilience enhance foster placement stability? A qualitative investigation." *International Journal of Psychological Studies 4*, 3, 153–167.

Radford, L., Corral, S., Bradley, C., Fisher, H., Bassett, C., Howat, N., and Collishaw S. (2011) *Child Abuse and Neglect in the UK Today.* London: NSPCC.

Raimondi, F., Capasso, L., Migliaro, F., Romano, A., and Paludetto, R. (2006) "Prenatal exposure to conjugated bilirubin." *Pediatrics 118*, 5, 2265.

Raslaviciene, G., and Zaborskis, A. (2002) "The development of mixed emotional and behavioral disorders in children raised in foster care institutions." *Medicina Kaunas Lithuania 38*, 7, 759–768.

Roque, L., and Veríssimo, M. (2011) "Emotional context, maternal behavior and emotion regulation." *Infant Behavior Development 34*, 4, 617–626.

Roy, K., Thiels, E., and Monaghan, A.P. (2002) "Loss of the *tailless* gene affects forebrain development and emotional behavior." *Physiology and Behavior 77*, 4–5, 595–600.

Rubin, D.M., O'Reilly, A.L.R., Luan, X., and Localio, A.R. (2007) "The impact of placement stability on behavioral well-being for children in foster care." *Pediatrics 119*, 2, 336–344.

Runyan, D.K., and Gould, C.L. (1985) "Foster care for child maltreatment: impact on delinquent behavior." *Pediatrics 75*, 3, 562–568.

Ryan, J.P., Testa, M.F., and Zhai, F. (2008) "African American males in foster care and the risk of delinquency: the value of social bonds and permanence." *Child Welfare 87*, 1, 115–140.

Saarni, C. (1997) "Emotional Competence and Self-regulation in Childhood." In P. Salovey and D.J. Sluyter (eds) *Emotional Development and Emotional Intelligence Educational Implications.* New York: Basic Books.

Salmon, A. (2010) "Using music to promote children's thinking and enhance their literacy development." *Early Child Development and Care 180*, 7, 937–945.

Sanders, M.R., Dadds, C.M., and Turner, K.M.T. (2003) "Theoretical, scientific and clinical foundations of the Triple P—Positive Parenting Program: a population approach to the promotion of parenting competence." *Parenting 1*, 1, 1–25.

Schneiderman, J.U. (2003) "Health issues of children in foster care." *Contemporary Nurse: A Journal for the Australian Nursing Profession 14*, 2, 123–128.

Schofield, G., and Beek, M. (2009) "Growing up in foster care: providing a secure base through adolescence." *Child and Family Social Work 14*, 3, 255–266.

Schofield, G., and Simmonds, J. (2011) "Contact for infants subject to care proceedings." *Adoption and Fostering 35*, 4, 70–74.

Schwartz, A. (2008) "Connective complexity: African American adolescents and the relational context of kinship foster care." *Child Welfare 87*, 2, 77–97.

Scott, J. (2011) "The impact of disrupted attachment on the emotional and interpersonal development of looked after children." *Educational and Child Psychology 28*, 3, 31–43.

Sheaffer, B.L., Golden, J.A., Bridgers, K.T., and Hall, C.W. (2009) "Nonverbal processing and social competency in children with reactive attachment disorder." *Behavior Development Bulletin 15*, 11–17.

Simmel, C. (2007) "Risk and protective factors contributing to the longitudinal psychosocial well-being of adopted foster children." *Journal of Emotional and Behavioral Disorders 15*, 4, 237–249.

Slowikowski, J., Finkelhor, D., Turner, H., and Hamby, S. (2011) *Polyvictimization: Children's Exposure to Multiple Types of Violence, Crime, and Abuse.* Office of Justice Program: National Survey of Children's Exposure to Violence. Washington, DC: US Department of Justice. Available at https://www.ncjrs.gov/pdffiles1/ojjdp/235504.pdf, accessed on 26 December 2012.

Smith, D.K., Leve, L.D., and Chamberlain, P. (2011) "Preventing internalizing and externalizing problems in girls in foster care as they enter middle school: impact of an intervention." *Prevention Science 12*, 3, 269–277.

Smith, D.K., Stormshak, E., Chamberlain, P., and Whaley, R.B. (2001) "Placement disruption in treatment foster care." *Journal of Emotional and Behavioral Disorders 9*, 3, 200–205.

Smith, J., and Boone, A. (2006) "Future outlook in African American kinship care families." *Journal of Health Social Policy 22*, 3–4, 9–30.

Smucker, K.S., Kauffman, J.M., and Ball, D.W. (1995) "School-related problems of special education foster care students with emotional or behavioral disorders: a comparison to other groups." *Journal of Emotional and Behavioral Disorders 4*, 1, 30–39.

Smyke, A.T., Zeanah, C.H., Fox, N.A., Nelson, C.A., and Guthrie, D. (2010) "Placement in foster care enhances quality of attachment among young institutionalized children." *Child Development 81*, 1, 212–223.

Sroufe, L.A. (1996a) *Emotional Development: The Organization of Emotional Life in the Early Years.* Cambridge Studies in Social Emotional Development. Cambridge: Cambridge University Press.

Sroufe, L.A. (1996b) "Emotional Development." In L. Carmichael (ed.) *Development.* Cambridge: Cambridge University Press.

Stovall, K.C., and Dozier, M. (2008) "Infants in foster care infants in foster care: an attachment theory perspective." *Adoption Quarterly 2*, 37–41.

Strijker, J., Knorth, E.J., and Knot-Dickscheit, J. (2008) "Placement history of foster children: a study of placement history and outcomes in long-term family foster care." *Child Welfare 87*, 5, 107–124.

Strijker, P., and Knorth, E.J. (2007) "First International Network Conference on Foster Care." In H. Grietens, E.J. Knorth, P. Durning, and J. Dumas (eds.) *Promoting Competence in Children and Families: Scientific Perspectives on Resilience and Vulnerablility,* 1–16. Leuven, Belgium: Leuven University Press.

Suinn, R.M. (2009) "Acculturation: Measurements and Review of Findings." In N.-H. Trinh, Y.C. Rho, F.G. Lu, and K.M. Sanders (eds) *Handbook of Mental Health and Acculturation in Asian American Families.* Totowa, NJ: Humana Press.

Tarren-Sweeney, M.J., Hazell, P.L., and Carr, V.J. (2004) "Are foster parents reliable informants of children's behaviour problems?" *Child Care Health and Development 30,* 2, 167–175.

Taussig, H.N., and Talmi, A. (2001) "Ethnic differences in risk behaviors and related psychosocial variables among a cohort of maltreated adolescents in foster care." *Child Maltreatment 6,* 2, 180–192.

Teisl, M., and Cicchetti, D. (2008) "Physical abuse, cognitive and emotional processes, and aggressive/disruptive behavior problems." *Social Development 17,* 1, 1–23.

The Brookdale Foundation Group (2010) *GrandFacts: United States.* Washington, DC: The Brookdale Foundation Group. Available at www.aarp.org/relationships/friends-family/grandfacts-sheets, accessed on 21 December 2012.

Thompson, H. (2011) "The experience of living with a foster sibling, as described by the birth children of foster carers: a thematic analysis of the literature." *Adoption and Fostering Journal 35,* 2, 49–60.

Thompson, R.G., and Auslander, W.F. (2011) "Substance use and mental health problems as predictors of HIV sexual risk behaviors among adolescents in foster care." *Health Social Work 36,* 1, 33–43.

Thrall, E.E., Hall, C.W., Golden, J.A., and Sheaffer, B.L. (2010) "Attachment disorder." *Behavior Development Bulletin 15,* 4–11.

Tubbs, N.R. (2002) "Special education and foster care: state policies leave foster children with disabilities unprotected in the special education system." *Children's Legal Bulletin,* Spring 2002. Available at www.kidlaw.org/main.asp?uri=1003&di=136.htm&dt=0&sti=2, accessed on 26 December 2012.

Tyebjee, T. (2003) "Attitude, interest, and motivation for adoption and foster care." *Child Welfare 82,* 6 685–706.

Ungar, M., and Perry, B.D. (2012) "Violence, Trauma, and Resilience." In R. Alaggia and C. Vine (eds) *Cruel But Not Unusual: Violence in Canadian Families.* Waterloo: Wilfred Laurier Press.

United States Government Accountability Office (2011) *Child Welfare: More Information and Collaboration Could Promote Ties Between Foster Care Children and Their Incarcerated Parents.* Washington, DC: Government Accountability Office.

University of California (2008) *Placement Stability in Child Welfare Services Issues, Concerns, Outcomes and Future Directions Literature Review.* Davis, CA: University of California.

US Department of Health and Human Services (n.d.) *Report to Congress on Kinship Foster Care.* Washington, DC: Dept of Health and Human Services. Available at http://aspe.hhs.gov/hsp/kinr2c00/full.pdf, accessed on 26 December 2012.

Valle, J.F., Bravo, A., and López, M. (2009) "Foster care in Spain: its establishment and current challenges." *Papeles Del Psicólogo 30,* 1, 33–41.

Van Andel, H.W.H., Grietens, H., and Knorth, E.K. (2012) "Foster carer—foster child intervention (FFI): an intervention designed to reduce stress in young children placed in a foster family." *Adoption and Fostering 36*, 2, 19–28.

Van Den Dries, L., Juffer, F., Van IJzendoorn, M.H., Bakermans-Kranenburg, M.J., and Alink, L.R. (2012) "Infants' responsiveness, attachment, and indiscriminate friendliness after international adoption from institutions or foster care in China: application of emotional availability scales to adoptive families." *Development and Psychopathology 24*, 1, 49–64.

Van IJzendoorn, M.H., and Sagi, A. (1999) "Cross Cultural Patterns of Attachment: Universal and Contextual Dimensions." In J. Cassidy and P.R. Shaver (eds) *Handbook of attachment: Theory, research, and clinical applications.* New York, NY: The Guilford Press.

Vaughn, M.G., Ollie, M.T., McMillen, J.C., Scott, L., and Munson, M. (2007) "Substance use and abuse among older youth in foster care." *Addictive Behaviors 32*, 9, 1929–1935.

Vaughn, M.G., Shook, J.J., and McMillen, J.C. (2008) "Aging out of foster care and legal involvement: toward a typology of risk." *Social Service Review 82*, 3, 419–446.

Votruba-Drzal, E., Coley, R.L., Maldonado-Carreño, C., Li-Grining, C.P., and Chase-Lansdale, P.L. (2010) "Child care and the development of behavior problems among economically disadvantaged children in middle childhood." *Child Development 81*, 3, 1460–1474.

Walker, J. (2008) "The use of attachment theory in adoption." *Adoption and Fostering 32*, 1, 49–58.

Washington, K.T. (2008) "Attachment and alternatives: theory in child welfare research." *Advances in Social Work 9*, 1, 8–16.

Webster-Stratton, C. (1991) "Annotation: Strategies for working with families of conduct disordered children." *British Journal of Child Psychiatry and Psychology* 32(7): 1047–1062.

Whyte, A., Job, D., Giles, S., and Lawrie, S. (2008) "Meeting curation challenges in a neuroimaging group." *International Journal of Digital Curation 3*, 1, 171–181.

Williams, L.M., and Gordon, E. (2007) "The neuroscientist dynamic organization of the emotional brain: responsivity, stability, and instability." *The Neuroscientist 13*, 4, 349–370.

Williams, N.J., and Sherr, M.E. (2008) "Children's psychosocial rehabilitation: clinical outcomes for youth with serious emotional disturbance living in foster care." *Child and Adolescent Social Work Journal 26*, 3, 225–234.

Wilson, K. (2006) "Can foster carers help children resolve their emotional and behavioural difficulties?" *Clinical Child Psychology and Psychiatry 11*, 4, 495–511.

Wolf, K. (2008) "Foster care research in Germany: a critical review." *Adoption and Fostering 32*, 2, 19–30.

Woo, B.S., Ng, T.P., Fung, D.S., Chan, Y.H., Lee, Y.P., Koh, J.B., and Cai Y. (2007) "Emotional and behavioural problems in Singaporean children based on parent, teacher and child reports." *Singapore Medical Journal 49*, 5, 439; author reply 440.

Woods, S.B., Farineau, H.M., and McWey, L.M. (2012) "Physical health, mental health, and behaviour problems among early adolescents in foster care." *Child Care Health Dev.* doi:10.1111/j.1365-2214.2011.01357.x.

Zima, B.T, Bussing, R., Freeman, S., Yang, X., Belin, T.R., and Forness, S.R. (2000) "Behavior problems, academic skill delays and school failure among school-aged children in foster care: their relationship to placement characteristics." *Journal of Child and Family Studies 9*, 1, 87–103.

Zionts, P., and Zionts, L. (1997) "Rational emotive behavior therapy with troubled students." *Reclaiming Children and Youth 6*, 2, 103–108.

Ziv, Y., Aviezer, O., Gini, M., Sagi, A., and Koren-Karie, N. (2000) "Emotional availability in the mother-infant dyad as related to the quality of infant-mother attachment relationship." *Attachment Human Development 2*, 2, 149–169.

Zuravin, S.J., Benedict, M., and Somerfield, M. (1993) "Child maltreatment in family foster care." *The American Journal of Orthopsychiatry 63*, 4, 589–596.

# ABOUT THE AUTHOR

Dr. Kalyani Gopal is a licensed clinical psychologist with over 25 years' experience in diverse clinical settings. Dr. Gopal began her doctoral training in clinical psychology in Vanderbilt University and completed her training at Alliant University. Her interests are in child sexual abuse assessment and treatment, expert witness testimony, long-term sequelae of child sexual abuse, juvenile delinquency, parenting, psychopathology, attachment issues, foster care assessment, adjustment, and training, media relations, and immigrant experiences. Dr. Gopal is on the Lake County Child Protection Team and the Lake County Child Fatality Team and was the recipient of the Outstanding Service to Lake County award in 2002. She currently holds the position as President and Clinical Director of Mid-America Psychological and Counseling Services in Merrillville, Indiana, and provides clinical supervision to five outpatient clinics in Indiana and Illinois. Dr. Gopal is an international speaker on Child Sexual Abuse and has conducted workshops across the country and internationally on the Impact of Child Sexual Abuse. Dr. Gopal is the President of the Clinical Psychology of Women (Section IV), Division of Clinical Psychology (12), American Psychological Association, and is the Illinois Psychological Association Statewide Advocate Coordinator for severe mental illness. Dr. Gopal is also the co-author of *Americanization of New Immigrants.*

# INDEX